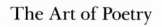

The Art of Poetry

POETS ON POETRY

DAVID LEHMAN, GENERAL EDITOR

A. R. Ammons *Set in Motion*
Douglas Crase *AMERIFIL.TXT*
Suzanne Gardinier *A World That Will Hold All the People*
Kenneth Koch *The Art of Poetry*

DONALD HALL, FOUNDING EDITOR

Martin Lammon, Editor
  Written in Water, Written in Stone
Philip Booth *Trying to Say It*
Joy Harjo *The Spiral of Memory*
Richard Tillinghast
  Robert Lowell's Life and Work
Marianne Boruch *Poetry's Old Air*
Alan Williamson *Eloquence and Mere Life*
Mary Kinzie *The Judge Is Fury*
Thom Gunn *Shelf Life*
Robert Creeley *Tales Out of School*
Fred Chappell *Plow Naked*
Gregory Orr *Richer Entanglements*
Daniel Hoffman *Words to Create a World*
David Lehman *The Line Forms Here*
  · *The Big Question*
Jane Miller *Working Time*
Amy Clampitt *Predecessors, Et Cetera*
Peter Davison
  One of the Dangerous Trades
William Meredith
  Poems Are Hard to Read
Tom Clark *The Poetry Beat*
William Matthews *Curiosities*
Charles Wright *Halflife* · *Quarter Notes*
Weldon Kees
  Reviews and Essays, 1936–55
Tess Gallagher *A Concert of Tenses*
Charles Simic *The Uncertain Certainty*
  · *Wonderful Words, Silent Truth*
  · *The Unemployed Fortune-Teller*
Anne Sexton *No Evil Star*
John Frederick Nims *A Local Habitation*

Donald Justice *Platonic Scripts*
Robert Hayden *Collected Prose*
Hayden Carruth *Effluences from the*
  Sacred Caves · *Suicides and Jazzers*
John Logan *A Ballet for the Ear*
Alicia Ostriker
  Writing Like a Woman
Marvin Bell *Old Snow Just Melting*
James Wright *Collected Prose*
Marge Piercy
  Parti-Colored Blocks for a Quilt
John Haines *Living Off the Country*
Philip Levine *Don't Ask*
Louis Simpson *A Company of Poets*
  · *The Character of the Poet*
  · *Ships Going into the Blue*
Richard Kostelanetz
  The Old Poetries and the New
David Ignatow *Open Between Us*
Robert Francis *Pot Shots at Poetry*
Robert Bly *Talking All Morning*
Diane Wakoski *Toward a New Poetry*
Maxine Kumin *To Make a Prairie*
Donald Davie *Trying to Explain*
William Stafford
  Writing the Australian Crawl ·
  You Must Revise Your Life
Galway Kinnell
  Walking Down the Stairs
Donald Hall *Goatfoot Milktongue*
  Twinbird · *The Weather for Poetry* ·
  Poetry and Ambition · *Death to the*
  Death of Poetry

Kenneth Koch

The Art of Poetry

POEMS,

PARODIES,

INTERVIEWS,

ESSAYS, AND

OTHER WORK

Ann Arbor
THE UNIVERSITY OF MICHIGAN PRESS

To John Ashbery

Copyright © by the University of Michigan 1996
All rights reserved
Published in the United States of America by
The University of Michigan Press
Manufactured in the United States of America
∞ Printed on acid-free paper

1999   1998   1997   1996   4   3   2   1

A CIP catalog record for this book is available from the British Library.

Library of Congress Cataloging-in-Publication Data

Koch, Kenneth, 1925–
   [Selections.   1996]
   The art of poetry : poems, parodies, interviews, essays, and other work
/ Kenneth Koch.
      p.   cm.   —   (Poets on poetry)
   ISBN 0-472-09605-2.—ISBN 0-472-06605-6 (pbk.)
   1. Koch, Kenneth, 1925–   —Interviews.   2. Authors,
American—20th century—Interviews.   3. Poetics.   I. Title.
II. Series.
PS3521.O27A6   1996
811'.54—dc20   96-42536
                                                                 CIP

Contents

An Introductory Note

I have written very little literary criticism, but literature, especially poetry, has often been a subject in whatever else I have written—poetry, plays, fiction. I spent a few years finding a way to teach schoolchildren to write poetry. I also did the same sort of investigation into teaching elderly people in a nursing home to write poetry. Now, later, it seems clear that the methods I discovered and what I wrote about these experiences express views about poetry: where it originates, what is good about it, what good it can do. So the contents of this book of "criticism" include two essays about teaching poetry to children and one chapter from a book about teaching poetry in a nursing home. There are two longish poems about poetry, one a protest, the other more calmly descriptive: "Fresh Air" and "The Art of Poetry." There are a number of parodies, all of poets whose work I like but felt slightly bothered by in one way or another. There are the manifestoes, memoirs, and poems of an imaginary literary movement, "Hasosismo"; a few short plays, and a conversation from a novel. There are two interviews, one about a specific work, a play, and the other more general. There are also a memoir, an introduction to a reading, a note about collaborative works with painters, and a talk about poetic influences. The few critical essays were written in response to work by writers I admired to such a degree that I wanted to explain my admiration.

—New York City, June 23, 1996

I

The Art of Poetry

To write a poem, perfect physical condition
Is desirable but not necessary. Keats wrote
In poor health, as did D. H. Lawrence. A combination
Of disease and old age is an impediment to writing, but
Neither is, alone, unless there is arteriosclerosis—that is,
Hardening of the arteries—but that we shall count as a
    disease
Accompanying old age and therefore a negative condition.
Mental health is certainly not a necessity for the
Creation of poetic beauty, but a degree of it
Would seem to be, except in rare cases. Schizophrenic poetry
Tends to be loose, disjointed, uncritical of itself, in some
    ways
Like what is best in our modern practice of the poetic art
But unlike it in others, in its lack of concern
For intensity and nuance. A few great poems
By poets supposed to be "mad" are of course known to us all,
Such as those of Christopher Smart, but I wonder how crazy
    they were,
These poets who wrote such contraptions of exigent art?
As for Blake's being "crazy," that seems to me very unlikely.

From *The Art of Love* (Random House, 1975).

But what about Wordsworth? Not crazy, I mean, but what
    about his later work, boring
To the point of inanity, almost, and the destructive "correc-
    tions" he made
To his *Prelude,* as it nosed along, through the shallows of art?
He was really terrible after he wrote the "Ode:
Intimations of Immortality from Recollections of Early Child-
    hood," for the most part,
Or so it seems to me. Walt Whitman's "corrections," too, of
    the *Leaves of Grass,*
And especially "Song of Myself," are almost always terrible.

Is there some way to ride to old age and to fame and
    acceptance
And pride in oneself and the knowledge society approves
    one
Without getting lousier and lousier and depleted of talent?
Yes, Yeats shows it could be. And Sophocles wrote poetry
    until he was a hundred and one,
Or a hundred, anyway, and drank wine and danced all
    night.
But he was an Ancient Greek and so may not help us here. On
The other hand, he may. There is, it would seem, a sense
In which one must grow and develop, and yet stay young—
Not peroxide, not stupid, not transplanting hair to look
    peppy,
But young in one's heart. And for this it is a good idea to
    have some
Friends who write as well as you do, who know what you are
    doing,
And know when you are doing something wrong.
They should have qualities that you can never have,
To keep you continually striving up an impossible hill.
These friends should supply such competition as will make
    you, at times, very uncomfortable.
And you should take care of your physical body as well
As of your poetic heart, since consecutive hours of advanced
    concentration
Will be precious to your writing and may not be possible

If you are exhausted and ill. Sometimes an abnormal or sick state
Will be inspiring, and one can allow oneself a certain number,
But they should not be the rule. Drinking alcohol is all right
If not in excess, and I would doubt that it would be beneficial
During composition itself. As for marijuana, there are those who
Claim to be able to write well under its influence
But I have yet to see the first evidence for such claims.
Stronger drugs are ludicrously inappropriate, since they destroy judgment
And taste, and make one either like or dislike everything one does,
Or else turn life into a dream. One does not write well in one's sleep.

As for following fashionable literary movements,
It is almost irresistible, and for a while I can see no harm in it,
But the sooner you find your own style the better off you will be.
Then all "movements" fit into it. You have an "exercycle" of your own.
Trying out all kinds of styles and imitating poets you like
And incorporating anything valuable you may find there,
These are sound procedures, and in fact I think even essential
To the perfection of an original style which is yours alone.
An original style may not last more than four years,
Or even three or even two, sometimes on rare occasions one,
And then you must find another. It is conceivable even that a style
For a very exigent poet would be for one work only,
After which it would be exhausted, limping, unable to sustain any wrong or right.
By "exigent" I mean extremely careful, wanting each poem to be a conclusion

Of everything he senses, feels, and knows.

The exigent poet has his satisfactions, which are relatively special

But that is not the only kind of poet you can be. There is a pleasure in being Venus,

In sending love to everyone, in being Zeus,

In sending thunder to everyone, in being Apollo

And every day sending out light. It is a pleasure to write continually

And well, and that is a special poetic dream

Which you may have or you may not. Not all writers have it.

Browning once wrote a poem every day of one year

And found it "didn't work out well." But who knows?

He went on for a year—something must have been working out.

And why only one poem a day? Why not several? Why not one every hour for eight to ten hours a day?

There seems no reason not to try it if you have the inclination.

Some poets like "saving up" for poems, others like to spend incessantly what they have.

In spending, of course, you get more, there is a "bottomless pocket"

Principle involved, since your feelings are changing every instant

And the language has millions of words, and the number of combinations is infinite.

True, one may feel, perhaps Puritanically, that

One person can only have so much to say, and, besides, ten thousand poems per annum

Per person would flood the earth and perhaps eventually the universe,

And one would not want so many poems—so there is a "quota system"

Secretly, or not so secretly, at work. "If I can write one good poem a year,

I am grateful," the noted Poet says, or "six" or "three." Well, maybe for that Poet,

But for you, fellow paddler, and for me, perhaps not. Be-
sides, I think poems
Are esthetecologically harmless and psychodegradable
And never would they choke the spirits of the world. For a
poem only affects us
And "exists," really, if it is worth it, and there can't be too
many of those.
Writing constantly, in any case, is the poetic dream
Diametrically opposed to the "ultimate distillation"
Dream, which is that of the exigent poet. Just how good a
poem should be
Before one releases it, either from one's own work or then
into the purview of others,
May be decided by applying the following rules: ask 1) Is it
astonishing?
Am I pleased each time I read it? Does it say something I
was unaware of
Before I sat down to write it? and 2) Do I stand up from it a
better man
Or a wiser, or both? or can the two not be separated? 3) Is it
really by me
Or have I stolen it from somewhere else? (This sometimes
happens,
Though it is comparatively rare.) 4) Does it reveal something
about me
I never want anyone to know? 5) Is it sufficiently "modern"?
(More about this a little later) 6) Is it in my own "voice"?
Along with, of course, the more obvious questions, such as
7) Is there any unwanted awkwardness, cheap effects, asking
illegitimately for attention,
Show-offiness, cuteness, pseudo-profundity, old hat checks,
Unassimilated dream fragments, or other "literary," "kiss-
me-I'm-poetical" junk?
Is my poem free of this? 8) Does it move smoothly and
swiftly
From excitement to dream and then come flooding reason
With purity and soundness and joy? 9) Is this the kind of
poem
I would envy in another if he could write? 10)

Would I be happy to go to Heaven with this pinned on to my
Angelic jacket as an entrance show? Oh, would I? And if you
    can answer to all these Yes
Except for the 4th one, to which the answer should be No,
Then you can release it, at least for the time being.
I would look at it again, though, perhaps in two hours, then
    after one or two weeks,
And then a month later, at which time you can probably be
    sure.

To look at a poem again of course causes anxiety
In many cases, but that pain a writer must learn to endure,
For without it he will be like a chicken that never knows what
    it is doing
And goes feathering and fluttering through life. When one
    finds the poem
Inadequate, then one must revise, and this can be very hard
    going
Indeed. For the original "inspiration" is not there. Some
    poets never master the
Art of doing this, and remain "minor" or almost nothing at
    all.
Such have my sympathy but not my praise. My sympathy
    because
Such work is difficult, and most persons accomplish nothing
    whatsoever
In the course of their lives; at least these poets are writing
"First versions," but they can never win the praise
Of a discerning reader until they take large-hearted Revision
    to bed
And win her to their cause and create through her "second-
    time-around" poems
Or even "third-time-around" ones. There are several ways to
    gain
The favors of this lady. One is unstinting labor, but be
    careful
You do not ruin what is already there by unfeeling rewriting
That makes it more "logical" but cuts out its heart.
Sometimes neglecting a poem for several weeks is best,

As if you had forgotten you wrote it, and changing it then
As swiftly as you can—in that way, you will avoid at least dry
    "re-detailing"
Which is fatal to any art. Sometimes the confidence you have
    from a successful poem
Can help you to find for another one the changes you want.
Actually, a night's sleep and a new day filled with confidence
    are very desirable,
And, once you get used to the ordinary pains that go with
    revising,
You may grow to like it very much. It gives one the strange
    feeling
That one is "working on" something, as an engineer does, or
    a pilot
When something goes wrong with the plane; whereas the
    inspired first version of a poem
Is more like simply a lightning flash to the heart.
Revising gives one the feeling of being a builder. And if it
    brings pain? Well,
It sometimes does, and women have pain giving birth to
    children
Yet often wish to do so again, and perhaps the grizzly bear
    has pain
Burrowing down into the ground to sleep all winter. In
    writing
The pain is relatively minor. We need not speak of it again
Except in the case of the fear that one has "lost one's talent,"
Which I will go into immediately. This fear
Is a perfectly logical fear for poets to have,
And all of them, from time to time, have it. It is very rare
For what one does best and that on which one's happiness
    depends
To so large an extent, to be itself dependent on factors
Seemingly beyond one's control. For whence cometh
    Inspiration?
Will she stay in her Bower of Bliss or come to me this
    evening?
Have I gotten too old for her kisses? Will she like that boy
    there rather than me?

Am I a dried-up old hog? Is this then the end of it?
    Haven't I
Lost that sweet easy knack I had last week,
Last month, last year, last decade, which pleased everyone
And especially pleased me? I no longer can feel the warmth
    of it—
Oh, I have indeed lost it! Etcetera. And when you write a
    new poem
You like, you forget this anguish, and so on till your death,
Which you'll be remembered beyond, not for "keeping your
    talent,"
But for what you wrote, in spite of your worries and fears.

The truth is, I think, that one does not lose one's talent,
Although one can misplace it—in attempts to remain in the
    past,
In profitless ventures intended to please those whom
Could one see them clearly one would not wish to please,
In opera librettos, or even in one's life
Somewhere. But you can almost always find it, perhaps in
    trying new forms
Or not in form at all but in the (seeming) lack of it—
Write "stream of consciousness." Or, differently again, do
    some translations.
Renounce repeating the successes of the years before. Seek
A success of a type undreamed of. Write a poetic fishing
    manual. Try an Art of Love.
Whatever, be on the lookout for what you feared you had
    lost,
The talent you misplaced. The only ways really to lose it
Are serious damage to the brain or being so attracted
To something else (such as money, sex, repairing expensive
    engines)
That you forget it completely. In that case, how care that it is
    lost?
In spite of the truth of all this, however, I am aware
That fear of lost talent is a natural part of a poet's
    existence.
So be prepared for it, and do not let it get you down.

Just how much experience a poet should have
To be sure he has enough to be sure he is an adequate
    knower
And feeler and thinker of experience as it exists in our
    time
Is a tough one to answer, and the only sure rule I can think
    of
Is experience as much as you can and write as much as you
    can.
These two can be contradictory. A great many experiences
    are worthless
At least as far as poetry is concerned. Whereas the least
    promising,
Seemingly, will throw a whole epic in one's lap. However,
    that is Sarajevo
And not cause. Probably. I do not know what to tell you
That would apply to all cases. I would suggest travel
And learning at least one other language (five or six
Could be a distraction). As for sexuality and other
Sensual pleasures, you must work that out for yourself.
You should know the world, men, women, space, wind,
    islands, governments,
The history of art, news of the lost continents, plants,
    evenings,
Mornings, days. But you must also have time to write.
You need environments for your poems and also people,
But you also need life, you need to care about these things
And these persons, and that is the difficulty, that
What you will find best to write about cannot be experienced
Merely as "material." There are some arts one picks up
Of "living sideways," and forwards and backwards at the
    same time,
But they often do not work—or do, to one's disadvantage:
You feel, "I did not experience that. That cow did
More than I. Or that 'Blue Man' without a thought in the world
Beyond existing. He is the one who really exists.
That is true poetry. I am nothing." I suggest waiting a few
    hours
Before coming to such a rash decision and going off

Riding on a camel yourself. For you cannot escape your mind
And your strange interest in writing poetry, which will make you,
Necessarily, an experiencer and un-experiencer
Of life at the same time, but you should realize that what you do
Is immensely valuable, and difficult, too, in a way riding a camel is not,
Though that is valuable too—you two will amaze each other,
The Blue Man and you, and that is also a part of life
Which you must catch in your poem. As for how much one's poetry
Should "reflect one's experience," I do not think it can avoid
Doing that. The naïve version of such a concern
Of course is stupid, but if you feel the need to "confront"
Something, try it, and see how it goes. To "really find your emotions,"
Write, and keep working at it. Success in the literary world
Is mostly irrelevant but may please you. It is good to have a friend
To help you past the monsters on the way. Becoming famous will not hurt you
Unless you are foolishly overcaptivated and forget
That this too is merely a part of your "experience." For those who make poets famous
In general know nothing about poetry. Remember your obligation is to write,
And, in writing, to be serious without being solemn, fresh without being cold,
To be inclusive without being asinine, particular
Without being picky, feminine without being effeminate,
Masculine without being brutish, human while keeping all the animal graces
You had inside the womb, and beast-like without being inhuman.
Let your language be delectable always, and fresh and true.
Don't be conceited. Let your compassion guide you

And your excitement. And always bring your endeavors to
  their end.

One thing a poem needs is to be complete
In itself and not need others to complement it.
Therefore this poem about writing should be complete
With information about everything concerned in the act
Of creating a poem. A work also should not be too long.
Each line should give a gathered new sensation
Of "Oh, now I know that, and want to go on!"
"Measure," which decides how long a poem should be,
Is difficult, because possible elaboration is endless,
As endless as the desire to write, so the decision to end
A poem is generally arbitrary yet must be made
Except in the following two cases: when one embarks on an
  epic
Confident that it will last all one's life,
Or when one deliberately continues it past hope of
  concluding—
Edmund Spenser and Ezra Pound seem examples
Of one of these cases or the other. And no one knows how
The Faerie Queene continued (if it did, as one writer said,
The last parts destroyed in the sacking of Spenser's house
By the crazed but justified Irish, or was it by his servants?).
It may be that Spenser never went beyond Book Six
In any serious way, because the thought of ending was
  unpleasant,
Yet his plan for the book, if he wrote on, would oblige him
  to end it. This unlike Pound
Who had no set determined place to cease. Coming to a stop
And giving determined form is easiest in drama,
It may be, or in short songs, like "We'll Go
No More a-Roving," one of Byron's most
Touching poems, an absolute success, the best
Short one, I believe, that Byron wrote. In all these
Cases, then, except for "lifetime" poems, there is a point one
  reaches
When one knows that one must come to an end,

And that is the point that must be reached. To reach it, however,
One may have to cut out much of what one has written along the way,
For the end does not necessarily come of itself
But must be coaxed forth from the material, like a blossom.

Anyone who would like to write an epic poem
May wish to have a plot in mind, or at least a mood—the
Minimum requirement is a form. Sometimes a stanza,
Like Spenser's, or Ariosto's ottava rima, will set the poem going
Downhill and uphill and all around experience
And the world in the maddest way imaginable. Enough,
In this case, to begin, and to let oneself be carried
By the wind of eight (or, in the case of Spenser, nine) loud rhymes.
Sometimes blank verse will tempt the amateur
Of endless writing; sometimes a couplet; sometimes "free verse."
"Skeltonics" are hard to sustain over an extended period
As are, in English, and in Greek for all I know, "Sapphics."
The epic has a clear advantage over any sort of lyric
Poem in being there when you go back to it to continue. The
Lyric is fleeting, usually caught in one
Breath or not at all (though see what has been said before
About revision—it can be done). The epic one is writing, however,
Like a great sheep dog is always there
Wagging and waiting to welcome one into the corner
To be petted and sent forth to fetch a narrative bone.
O writing an epic! what a pleasure you are
And what an agony! But the pleasure is greater than the agony,
And the achievement is the sweetest thing of all. Men raise the problem,
"How can one write an epic in the modern world?" One can answer,

"Look around you—tell me how one cannot!" Which is more
or less what
Juvenal said about Satire, but epic is a form
Our international time-space plan cries out for—or so it
seems
To one observer. The lyric is a necessity too,
And those you may write either alone
Or in the interstices of your epic poem, like flowers
Crannied in the Great Wall of China as it sweeps across the
earth.
To write only lyrics is to be sad, perhaps,
Or fidgety, or overexcited, too dependent on circumstance—
But there is a way out of that. The lyric must be bent
Into a more operative form, so that
Fragments of being reflect absolutes (see for example the
verse of
William Carlos Williams or Frank O'Hara), and you can go
on
Without saying it all every time. If you can master the knack
of it,
You are a fortunate poet, and a skilled one. You should read
A great deal, and be thinking of writing poetry all the time.
Total absorption in poetry is one of the finest things in
existence—
It should not make you feel guilty. Everyone is absorbed in
something.
The sailor is absorbed in the sea. Poetry is the mediation of
life.

The epic is particularly appropriate to our contemporary
world
Because we are so uncertain of everything and also know too
much,
A curious and seemingly contradictory condition, which the
epic salves
By giving us our knowledge and our grasp, with all our lack
of control as well.
The lyric adjusts to us like a butterfly, then epically eludes
our grasp.

Poetic drama in our time seems impossible but actually exists
    as
A fabulous possibility just within our reach. To write drama
One must conceive of an answerer to what one says, as I am
    now conceiving of you.

As to whether or not you use rhyme and how "modern" you
    are
It is something your genius can decide on every morning
When you get out of bed. What a clear day! Good luck at it!
Though meter is probably, and rhyme too, probably, dead
For a while, except in narrative stanzas. You try it out.
The pleasure of the easy inflection between meter and these
    easy vocable lines
Is a pleasure, if you are able to have it, you are unlikely to
    renounce.
As for "surrealistic" methods and techniques, they have
    become a
Natural part of writing. Your poetry, if possible, should be
    extended
Somewhat beyond your experience, while still remaining
    true to it;
Unconscious material should play a luscious part
In what you write, since without the unconscious part
You know very little; and your plainest statements should be
Even better than plain. A reader should put your work down
    puzzled,
Distressed, and illuminated, ready to believe
It is curious to be alive. As for your sense of what good you
Do by writing, compared to what good statesmen, doctors,
Flower salesmen, and missionaries do, perhaps you do less
And perhaps more. If you would like to try one of these
Other occupations for a while, try it. I imagine you will find
That poetry does something they do not do, whether it is
More important or not, and if you like poetry, you will like
    doing that yourself.

Poetry need not be an exclusive occupation.
Some think it should, some think it should not. But you
    should

Have years for poetry, or at least if not years months
At certain points in your life. Weeks, days, and hours may
   not suffice.
Almost any amount of time suffices to be a "minor poet"
Once you have mastered a certain amount of the craft
For writing a poem, but I do not see the good of minor
   poetry,
Like going to the Tour d'Argent to get dinner for your dog,
Or "almost" being friends with someone, or hanging around
   but not attending a school,
Or being a nurse's aide for the rest of your life after getting
   a degree in medicine,
What is the point of it? And some may wish to write songs
And use their talent that way. Others may even end up writ-
   ing ads.
To those of you who are left, when these others have
   departed,
And you are a strange bunch, I alone address these words.

It is true that good poetry is difficult to write.
Poetry is an escape from anxiety and a source of it as well.
On the whole, it seems to me worthwhile. At the end of a
   poem
One may be tempted to grow too universal, philosophical,
   and vague
Or to bring in History, or the Sea, but one should not do
   that
If one can possibly help it, since it makes
Each thing one writes sound like everything else,
And poetry and life are not like that. Now I have said
   enough.

Saint-John Perse's New Book

Amers is an epic poem in which the same thing happens on every page. But since what happens is the rebirth of beauty and life, and since this always happens in a different way, the poem is continually gorgeous and exciting, like twenty-five views of the sea in twenty-five places. It is all force, expanse, tragedy, and joy. This joy is the strangest thing about the poem—strangest for our time—and the best. Perse, by going, and staying, so close to the sources and secret currents of language cannot fail to acknowledge (fail! he is overwhelmed by it) the instinctive and recurring joy that is tied to speech. And the music of *Amers* is magnificent.

The problem for American readers is that Perse's French is very difficult; and one really should read him in French. So much depends on his language, his sounds, his shiftings of syntax that in his most noble and complex poems (of which *Amers* is one) he is as difficult to translate as Racine. But he must be read. His work in general and *Amers* in particular has qualities that American poetry cannot afford to ignore.

1) Size. *Amers* is a great big poem in which one has an impression of perfect control. It's like the sea, of course, and always a fresh breeze blowing.
2) His distance. A delicious politeness which objectifies everything in the world. It gives an impression of inhumanity and of the warmest humanity at the same time. Around the hero, Nietzsche said, everything becomes a tragedy; and around God everything becomes a world. Around Perse

From *Evergreen Review* 2, no. 7 (winter, 1959).

everything becomes his poetry—a strange sort of epic in which there is no advance, in which one is always at the peaks of imaginative excitement—"As if," Jouve wrote, "(he) were emptying his treasury at every instant." Perse's exquisite courtesy has nothing to do with "good manners": it is a positive quality, an attitude toward experience that is, despite the apparent contradiction, as frighteningly engaged as any attitude can be. That courtesy, that living on the heights from which one sees the world that makes one's heart hammer, how completely one feels the solitude and exile from which it comes! But Perse is no Tonio Kroger, artist exiled from society, who gazes with shame and desire at plump blonde people dancing; his window opens on the world

> Les promontoires aileés s'ouvrent au loin leur voie
> d'écume bleuissante.
> It is from the world itself that he seems (like everyone else)
> to be an exile; and his realization of the distance he must
> keep from it allows him to view it, as he recreates it, with all
> its horizons.

3) The choral technique; or cantata; or grand libretto. Poetesses, prophets, lovers, le Maître des étoiles et du Navigation, all have a chance to sing in praise of the sea. One feels them moving, one hears their voices, which in their changes are like the sea, like the imagination at its freest and most inspired.

4) Its music. Much good it does to commend it. I should imagine it could come only from an imagination that can be thrilled at every instant. It's quite extraordinary: "Ainsi Celle qui a nom frappe à midi le coeur éblouissant des eaux: Istar, splendide et nue, éperonée d'éclairs et d'aigles verts, dans les grands gazes vertes de son feu d'épaves . . . "

5) Its metaphors. Completely accurate (Perse doesn't speak of a parrot without knowing what its feathers feel like and how hard its beak is) and at the same time as wild and strong and free as those of any poet I know of. On every page they astonish, as of course they must if they are to please, and they satisfy as well; they create a desire and fulfill it at the same time: "Immense l'aube appelée mer, immense l'éten-

due des eaux, et sur la terre faite songe à nos confins violets,
toute la houle au loin quise lève et se couronne d'hyacinthes
comme un peuple d'amants!"

I suggest that American poetry can profit from Perse (even
more than it already has)—from the courage of his large de-
signs, from his insistence on reascending again and again the
heights of the heights, from his clear eye and from his sweep-
ing imagination. No one who reads Perse can fail, at the very
least, to realize that it has been possible to write (in the 1950s)
a poem so fantastic and so dazzlingly beautiful that one can
hardly believe it's there. Really, one has to rub one's eyes and,
with the mixed feelings that usually accompany such trials,
breathlessly look again. But it is there . . .

Mon amour, as-tu soif? Je suis femme à tes levres plus neuve
que la soif.

What has been sometimes grand and strong and sometimes
a little dreary about twentieth-century American poetry is its
closeness to reality, especially to historical reality, and with this
latter the tendency to criticize the present in light of the past.
The present is viewed in light of the past and alas! not much is
made of the present. What makes William Carlos Williams's
poems so odd and exciting, I think, is that they catch the music
of a man alive in his time with his hand on a table, his feet on the
floor, and his soul in the stars. But Williams is interested in the
source of the imagination rather than in the limits of the imagi-
nation, and different in this regard from Perse.

Any serious poetic statement about the past must take into
account the history of the imagination; but to exalt the imagina-
tion of the past without exploring that of the present is in a way
dishonest and useless. We cannot know anything about the past
unless we know about the present. The achievement of Perse, I
believe, is to have explored to its limits the possibility of exalta-
tion and joy in our time, and to have found them tremendous,
astounding, and grand. No one can call it a small discovery. We
have had, in this century, in America, poets with "the courage
to stare into the abyss"; couldn't we use some with the courage
to look Beauty in the eye and to tell the truth?

A Note on Frank O'Hara in the Early Fifties

The first thing of Frank O'Hara's I ever read was a story in the Harvard *Advocate* in 1948. It was about some people drunkenly going up stairs. During the next year, when I was living in New York, John Ashbery told me that Frank had started to write poems and that they were very good. I forget if I met Frank before or after John told me he had started writing poems. Actually, as I later found out, Frank had started writing poetry a long time before, and prose was only a temporary deviation for him. In any case, the first time I read some of Frank's poems was in the summer of 1950, just before I left for France on a Fulbright fellowship. John Ashbery had mailed them to me and had described them enthusiastically. I didn't like them very much. I wrote back to John that Frank was not as good as we were, and gave a few reasons why. These poems by Frank were somehow packed in one of my suitcases when I went abroad, and I happened to read them again when I was in Aix-en-Provence. This time they seemed to me marvelous; I was very excited about them. Also very intimidated. I believe I liked them for the same reasons I had not liked them before—i.e., because they were sassy, colloquial, and full of realistic detail.

It was not till the summer of 1952 (after coming back from Europe, I had gone to California for a year) that I got to know Frank well. *Know* is not really the right word, since it suggests something fairly calm and intellectual. This was something

From *Audit* (April 1964).

much more emotional and wild. Frank in his first two years in New York was having this kind of explosive effect on a lot of people that he met. Larry Rivers later said that Frank had a way of making you feel you were terribly important and that this was very inspiring, which is true, but it was more than that. His presence and his poetry made things go on around him which could not have happened in the same way if he hadn't been there. I know this is true of my poetry; and I would guess it was true also of the poetry of James Schuyler and John Ashbery, and of the painting of Jane Freilicher, Larry Rivers, Mike Goldberg, Grace Hartigan, and other painters too.

One of the most startling things about Frank in the period when I first knew him was his ability to write a poem when other people were talking, or even to get up in the middle of a conversation, get his typewriter, and write a poem, sometimes participating in the conversation while doing so. This may sound affected when I describe it, but it wasn't so at all. The poems he wrote in this way were usually very good poems. I was electrified by his ability to do this and at once tried to do it myself—(with considerably less success).

Frank and I collaborated on a birthday poem for Nina Castelli (summer, 1952), a sestina. This was the first time I had written a poem with somebody else and also the first time I had been able to write a good sestina (my earlier attempts had always bogged down in mystery and symbolism). Artistic collaboration, like writing a poem in a crowded room, is something that seemed to be a natural part of Frank's talent. I put this in the past tense not because these things are not part of Frank's talent now, but for the sake of history—since I believe that, as far as American poetry is concerned, he started something. Something about Frank that impressed me during the composition of the sestina was his feeling that the silliest idea actually in his head was better than the most profound idea actually in somebody else's head—which seems obvious once you know it, but how many poets have lived how many total years without ever finding it out?

This Nina Sestina collaboration occurred during one of the weekends in the summer of 1952 when Frank and I, Jane

Freilicher, Larry Rivers, and various other writers and painters were in East Hampton. Jane and Frank were sporadically engaged in being in a movie which was being made out there by John Latouche.

Frank's most famous poem during that summer was "Hatred," a rather long poem which he had typed up on a very long piece of paper which had been part of a roll. Another of his works which burst on us all like a bomb then was "Easter," a wonderful, energetic, and rather obscene poem of four or five pages, which consisted mainly of a procession of various bodily parts and other objects across a vast landscape. It was like Lorca and Whitman in some ways, but very original. I remember two things about it which were new: one was the phrase "the roses of Pennsylvania," and the other was the line in the middle of the poem which began "It is Easter!" (Easter, though it was the title, had not been mentioned before in the poem and apparently had nothing to do with it.) What I saw in these lines was 1) inspired irrelevance which turns out to be relevant (once Frank had said "It is Easter!" the whole poem was obviously about death and resurrection); 2) the use of movie techniques in poetry (in this case coming down hard on the title in the middle of a work); 3) the detachment of beautiful words from traditional contexts and putting them in curious new American ones ("roses of Pennsylvania").

He also mentioned a lot of things just because he liked them—for example, jujubes. Some of these things had not appeared before in poetry. His poetry contained aspirin tablets, Good Teeth buttons, and water pistols. His poems were full of passion and life; they weren't trivial because small things were called in them by name.

Frank and I both wrote long poems in 1953 (*Second Avenue* and *When the Sun Tries to Go On*). I had no clear intention of writing a 2400-line poem (which it turned out to be) before Frank said to me, on seeing the first 72 lines—which I regarded as a poem by itself—"Why don't you go on with it as long as you can?" Frank at this time decided to write a long poem too; I can't remember how much his decision to write such a poem had to do with his suggestion to me to write mine. While we were writing our long poems, we would read each other the results daily over the telephone. This seemed to inspire us a good deal.

Frank was very polite and also very competitive. Sometimes he gave other people his own best ideas, but he was quick and resourceful enough to use them himself as well. It was almost as though he wanted to give his friends a head start and was competitive partly to make up for this generosity. One day I told Frank I wanted to write a play, and he suggested that I, like no other writer living, could write a great drama about the conquest of Mexico. I thought about this, but not for too long, since within three or four days Frank had written his play *Awake in Spain*, which seemed to me to cover the subject rather thoroughly.

Something Frank had that none of the other artists and writers I know had to the same degree was a way of feeling and acting as though being an artist were the most natural thing in the world. Compared to him everyone else seemed a little self-conscious, abashed, or megalomaniacal. This natural-ness I think was really quite strange in New York in 1952. Frank's poetry had and has this same kind of ease about the fact that it exists and that it is so astonishing.

All the Imagination Can Hold

Frank O'Hara's work has already influenced a generation of young poets; some of those who are not poets may find it hard to judge the importance of what he has done when critics so often mistake solemnity for seriousness, obscurity for profundity, and the expression of pain for intensity of feeling. O'Hara's poems are buoyant, exuberant, wild, personal, open in troubling and troublesome ways, sometimes humorous, often about seemingly ordinary or trivial things, and radically original in form. They are the result of an unfamiliar aesthetic assumption: that what is really right there, in the poet's thoughts, fantasies, and feelings, is what is richest in possibility and worth the most attention. Beginning with whatever is there, if one's feelings are stirred by it, is the best way to get anywhere—

> That's not a cross look it's a sign of life
> but I'm glad you care how I look at you

In a book of twenty or thirty poems, certain of Frank O'Hara's subjects (lunch, movies) could seem trivial and willful because chosen at the expense of others; in this book of five hundred poems what strikes one is the breadth, sincerity, and exuberance of his concern for life. At first overwhelming, it is also liberating: by caring so much for so many things, he gives us back feelings of our own and permits us to respect

Review of *The Collected Poems of Frank O'Hara*, edited by Donald Allen from *The New Republic* (Jan. 1–8, 1972).

them. Garbo and Aphrodite are connected, but an exclusivist Yeatsian poetry can say only that they are one (like Maud Gonne and Helen of Troy) or that one is a cheapened version of the other. Frank O'Hara's poetry gives us the freedom to respond to both—as we do anyway, but not so much before he showed us how.

The honesty and immediacy of the poems are communicated in a verse which has seemingly learned plainness from Williams, variety from Pound, grandeur from Whitman, and music from all three; the result is a poetic line with more capability for drama, more flexibility, and more delicacy in rendering nuances of the speaking voice than any I know in modern poetry. It takes a whole poem to hear it right, but the conclusion of "Ballad" may give an idea:

> you know that I don't want to know you
> because the palm stands in the window disgusted
> by being transplanted, she feels that she's been outraged and she has
> by well-wisher me, she well wishes that I leave her alone and my self alone
> but tampering
> where does it come from? childhood? it seems good
> because it brings back the that
> that which we wish that which we want
> that which a ferry can become can become a bicycle if it wants to get
> across the river
> and doesn't care how
> though you will remember a night
> where nothing happened
> and we both were simply that
> and we loved each other so
> and it was unusual

In this poem, as in others, the movement seems determined by a musical line of feeling rather than by an intellectual working out or a preconceived form. It is as if the poet were writing to his feelings, as one might write poetry while listening to Chopin, letting the melodic rise and fall of the sound determine what one says. Frank O'Hara did in fact write some of his poems while listening to music; the immediacy of the relationship of what is happening outside to what happens in the poem is characteristic.

Frank O'Hara wrote his poems quickly, unexpectedly stirred by something he was thinking or feeling, often when other people were around. The speed and accidental aspect of his writing are not carelessness but are essential to what the poems are about: the will to catch what is there while it is really there and still taking place—

> I better hurry and finish this
> before your 3rd goes off the radio
> or I won't know what I'm feeling. . . .
> ("On Rachmaninoff's Birthday #158")

There is a difference between a feeling seized rapidly, while it's happening, or while it's being created (for his poems create feelings as much as they expose them) and a feeling considered in any other way. In catching a feeling in the process of coming into being, or as it first explodes into a thousand refractions, one can hope to reveal some of the truth that lies hidden in our unconscious, in all the things we have known or felt but can't be aware of simultaneously. The form of Frank O'Hara's poetry is flexible and consistently experimental— flexible, to accommodate the poem to whatever is taking place; experimental, perhaps for a number of reasons, among them to help awaken, by strangeness of form, new perceptions while he is writing.

For all their use of chance and the unconscious, Frank O'Hara's poems are unlike surrealist poetry in that they do not programmatically favor these forces (along with dreams and violence) over the intellectual and the conscious. He must have felt the power and beauty of unconscious phenomena in surrealist poems, but what he does is to use this power and beauty to ennoble, complicate, and simplify waking actions. His poems are like atoms for peace rather than for war; he brings unusual powers to everyday activities. His inability, or unwillingness, to stay in the realm of dreams and superpowers, stated explicitly at the end of "Sleeping on the Wing," is everywhere evident in his work.

                                                And, swooping,
       you relinquish all that you have made your own,
       the kingdom of your self sailing, for you must awake
       and breathe your warmth in this beloved image
       whether it's dead or merely disappearing,
       as space is disappearing and your singularity.

Of course it was not only the speed, spontaneity, and imme-
diacy with which Frank O'Hara wrote which enabled him to
write this poetry. It is a method of composition to surprise a
confusion of riches—but the riches have to be there. Without
them, poems written this way can seem like surprise raids on
empty buildings. Along with his brilliant intellect and his
wide-ranging knowledge of music, dance, art, history, and
philosophy, Frank O'Hara had an ability to fantasize himself
into being almost anybody, anything, anytime, anywhere; and
he also had an unusual gift for friendship and for love, for
identifying himself with, and for transforming other people
and their concerns. None of which detracted of course from
his passionate concern about himself and his own life, and
about all this he was always thinking, meditating "in an emer-
gency." It was always an emergency because one's life had to
be experienced and reflected on at the same time, and that is
just about impossible. He does it in his poems. The richness of
his perceptions gives the poems their characteristic dazzle:

       kisses! kisses!
       fresher than the river that runs like a moon through girls
       . . . .
       alfalfa blowing against sisters in a hanky of shade
                                                        ("Easter")

       What spanking opossums of sneaks are caressing the routes!
                                                ("Second Avenue")

The most ordinary things are presented with enough com-
plexity to make them real—

       an enormous party mesmerizing comers in the disgathering
          light
                                                ("Joe's Jacket")

and the most complex things are said as simply as possible:

> it is all enormity and life it has protected me and kept me
>   here on
> many occasions as a symbol does when the heart is full and
>   risks no speech
> a precaution I loathe as the pheasant loathes the season and is
>   preserved
> it will not be need, it will be just what it is and just what
>   happens

("Joe's Jacket")

The richness and agility of his mind can be seen clearly in his images, which tend to be instantaneous, immediately changing into something else, as in the first stanza of "Sleeping on the Wing" or in these lines from a slightly earlier poem:

>   he is throwing
> up his arms in heavenly desperation, spacious Y of his
> tumultuous love-nerves flailing like a poinsettia in
> its own nailish storm against the glass door of the
> cumulus which is withholding her from these divine
> pastures she has filled with the flesh of men as stones!

("Blocks")

The effect can be a crowding and a brightness which are "more than the ear can hold," as Frank O'Hara wrote of an orange bed in a painting by Willem de Kooning, and almost more than the imagination can hold, but not quite. One's feeling of being overwhelmed gives way to a happy awareness of expanded powers of perceiving and holding in mind.

The *Collected Poems* cover a period of eighteen years (1948–66). They move in general from being experience-inspired outbursts of imaginative creation to being imaginative illuminations of ordinary experience. What we see at first is a brilliant talent finding and testing itself in art, music, literature, and history, as well as in relations with a few friends. There is an atmosphere of continual invention and excited experimentation with form. During the first years in New York (1952–54), unhappiness and despair come into the poetry as they hadn't before, and with them a kind of toughness and defiance and the creation of rugged, hard, brilliant, surfacey kind of poems ("Easter," "Hatred," "Invincibility," "Life on Earth," *Second Avenue*) which in some ways resemble the big abstract canvasses Pollock, de Kooning, and others were painting at that time ("Easter" and *Second Avenue* seem to me among the wonders of contemporary poetry)—

> My hands are Massimo Plaster, called "White Pin in the Arm
>   of the Sea"
> and I'm blazoned and scorch like a fleet of windbells down
>   the Pulaski Skyway,
> table tops of Vienna carrying their bundles of cellophane to
>   the laundry,
> ear to the tongue, glistening semester of ardency, young-old
>   daringnesses
> at the foot of the most substantial art product of our times,
> the world; the jongleurs, fields of dizzyness. . . .
>
> *(Second Avenue)*

Like many of the shorter poems, these long poems seem composed at high speed, as if they were attempts to catch an infinite succession of moments or the infinite expansion of one. They are all in one breath—or in a series of breaths, each held as long as possible. In the late fifties there is a different kind of poem ("In Memory of My Feelings," "Ode to Michael Goldberg"), more introspective and directly autobiographical, more modulated in tone. Also of this period are many of what Frank O'Hara called his "I do this, I do that" poems, such as "The Day Lady Died," "Personal Poem," "A Step Away from Them." These are followed (1959–61) by a number of wonderfully tender and delicate love poems—such as "Les Luths," "St. Paul and all That," "Poem: Hate is only one of many responses." He wrote about them, "everything is too comprehensible / these are my delicate and caressing poems" ("Avenue A"). In the sixties there is the amazing "Biotherm," countless days with all their thoughts and sensations jammed into one rapidly shifting and unstopping statement, and shorter poems like it, such as "Maundy Saturday" and "New Particles from the Sun."

The changing character of the poems, however, is less remarkable than the energy and the vision that are everywhere present in them. The *Collected Poems* shows these qualities better than a shorter volume could: the range of Frank O'Hara's enterprise as a poet is so important a part, finally, of his work's value. It is a great experience to read it all. I have known Frank O'Hara's work for about twenty years and I had read a great many of the poems before. One reaction I had to this book, though, was astonishment. All those "moments," all the momentary enthusiasms and despairs which I had been moved by when I first read them, when they were here all together made something I had never imagined. It is not all one great poem, but something in some ways better: a collection of created moments that illuminate a whole life. Historically, his work seems to me to represent the last stage in the adaptation of twentieth-century avant-garde sensibility to poetry about contemporary American experience. In its music and its language and in its conception of the relation of poetry to the rest of life, it is a poetry which has already changed poets and others, and which promises to go on moving and changing them for a long time to come.

Poetry as Prose

James Schuyler, who is a poet, has written a remarkable novel. A casual glance—at an illustrated page, at the cover, at the blurb—is likely to give one as false an idea of what his book is about as the *New York Times* book review section evidently had when it treated this exquisitely comic work of art as a children's book which was good fun. *Alfred and Guinevere* does, in fact, tell the story of a few months in the lives of two children, a brother and sister. *Pride and Prejudice* is about a dance, a carriage ride, some rural marriage arrangements; and *Moby Dick* is about a whale. Mr. Schuyler's book is witty, truthful, simple, lively, and musical. One has to go to the really best poems of our time to find writing with as much skill in language, rhythm, refrain, the whole paraphernalia of poetry, as one finds here. The whole aim of the book is poetic—as though its author had set out to write a novel which would never violate for a moment his ear, his eye, his sensibility. The problem for poets writing novels is that they become bored (and so do readers), but Mr. Schuyler has transferred the excitements of poetry to his prose; something (witty or prosodic) is happening at every second. It is NOT, not at all, "poetic prose"—any more than is Jane Austen's. It is, rather, prose as poetry really should be: among other things fresh, surprising, artful, and clear; and with a great deal of its joy and shock arising from language—as in

---

Review of *Alfred and Guinevere,* by James Schuyler. From *Poetry* 93, no. 5 (February 1959).

What did I find everybody hunting high and low for Alfred and our poor dear old Grandmother who deserves a better fate more dead than alive in the kitchen a total wreck.

Who else can make poetry out of clichés? John Betjeman, but not the same. Sometimes one word brings a whole passage to life:

Betty and I set out following Stanley and Alfred in the A.M. but two boys followed us. They will be in my class if I go to school here next year. We disdained them, but Alfred and Stanley got away—

where *disdained* is a wonder—perfectly heard and at the same time odd. Schuyler's language makes one aware not only of what it describes, but also of language itself—of the word as a word among words—as poetry does, or should. His originality is in the way he uses this technique for the creation of comedy; musicality, as well as psychological accuracy, goes along with it. Part of Guinevere's diary:

Am almost finished reading Madame Bovary by Flaubert. It is very good for showing up people for what they are really like but not for story. I guess Marguerite de Valois will always be my favorite book. She is my ideal. Am always sucking in my cheeks so I will get to look more like her.

Now to bed. I am in bed already that means I will stop writing and read.

I will never get over the snooping. It is just like Madame Bovary by Flaubert.

Farther on, the "Bovary" refrain returns:

Finished Madame Bovary by Flaubert last night. The part where she buys the poison and dies is very true to life. How horrible to live and die in a small town and never have anybody understand you.

And

It rained all night and all day and it is still raining. How horrible—

a new refrain, "How horrible," which takes one back, makes music, but first of all—in its full context—makes one laugh. Which is, of course, the true test of comedy—who, if it failed, would care about its artistry? *Alfred and Guinevere* is not an easy book to discuss; I laughed all the way through it for three readings in a row—and wholeheartedly, as one can only laugh at something that is also beautiful. It is easier to quote. There are some marvelous descriptions of literature:

> . . . Anyway in the end he comes back to get even with the mean stepfather and there's a real scary part about a Bible in a cave. Only by then it turns out Rolf is all grown up and lean like a wild animal . . .

> . . . Well, one black, creepy, foggy night a long, long time ago before they had street lamps and you couldn't see where you were going . . .

and of Guinevere herself (by Guinevere):

> G. G., Guinevere Gates, Daughter of Samuel and Lucille Gates of this city and named for the beautiful legendary queen. After startling the capital cities of the world in her debut as a prodigy toe dancer, she opened her renowned custom clothes house in Paris, Guinevere Gowns, where she models her own designs . . .

and

> Some people would be very surprised if I just sailed away one day and was next heard from in India under the pen name of Sister Mary Guinevere silently living for others and passing on at an early age. From a dread disease. That would set them back on their heels.
> There is always nursing. That is a lot like being a nun. Except I would not want to spend my life walking around in big white shoes . . .

The book consists wholly of dialogue and diary and is, among other things, a parody of the completely objective style. In its apparent simplicity it is related to the kind of pure, clear, conscious prose that one finds in some Gertrude Stein and in early Hemingway, but it has a humor and a music that are quite its own.

The Poetry of Michel Deguy

I first read Michel Deguy's poems in Paris in 1969. I asked Eugène Guillevic, whom I had met in New York, what younger French poets I should read. "Deguy," he said, and I got a copy of *Ouï dire*. I read the poem that begins:

> Vous serez étonnées d'entendre la liberté de Paul
> Corinthiens II; 11, 19–33, 12, 1–9

I was interested, by its prosiness, its starting seemingly from nowhere, its slightly rough but hesitant music:

> N'gao sud-ouest où dorment les maîtresses
> Parmi le grain que couvent les grains
> Luther et les bardes N'zakara
> Tombes d'accord sur la cuisine[1]

It was something I hadn't seen before in French poetry.

The French poetry I knew best was the poetry in the great avant-garde tradition from Baudelaire and Rimbaud up through René Char. Despite its enormous variety, there were,

---

From *Given, Giving* (U. of California Press, 1984).

1. You will be astonished to hear the freedom of Paul Corinthians II: 11, 19–33; 12, 1–9

> (N'gao southwest where the mistresses sleep
> Among grain which is hatched by the grain
> Luther and the N'zakara bards
> Fall into agreement on cuisine)

in this poetry, certain similarities in tone and theme. Deguy's poems seemed obviously connected to this tradition, but just as obviously to break with it. His subjects; the roughness and prosiness of his music; the inclusion of odd words, rare, scientific, foreign, even of numerals; the changes in tone; the air of being unfinished and unresolved—all this gave a new kind of pleasure and suggested a somewhat different assumption about poetry. For all the differences, the poetry of Rimbaud, Éluard, Reverdy, and others had in common an inclination toward the irrational and the unconscious, away from reasoning and ordinary observation and toward dreams, visions, and strong sensations. Rimbaud believed the real truth was hidden in such places, as did Breton, and that this truth, if poetry could find it, could change the world. Other poets may simply have found the belief in, or search for, such a truth the best way to write poems. Intellect and rationality seemed no help, and in fact, they seemed impediments. Dreams, hallucinations, desires, and so on, were a way to escape them, as was writing, if not "automatically," at least with a very limited conscious control over what one was saying. It is as though poetry were thought of as a separate power, which, aided by such procedures, could go beyond any possible trajectory of intellect. Other ways of getting at the truth—intellectual ones, such as psychology, linguistics, and history—could only be thought of as mistaken paths. The tone of this poetry often has something in common with the tone of revelation—lyrical, often passionate, unified, uninterrupted; the tone of someone who has found out a secret truth, *the* truth—the truth of embracing the summer dawn (Rimbaud), of experiencing the light and shadow on a street (Reverdy).

Deguy's work doesn't show the same confidence in the world of dreams, sensation, and the unconscious. He is interested in how his predecessors wrote—unexpected transitions, confidence in momentary sensations, willingness to remain unclear—but not in their conclusions. The unconscious, the irrational, isn't the answer. The intellect or, perhaps more precisely, intellectual disciplines, such as psychology and linguistics, come back in his poetry. They come back as directions and as points of view and, verbally, as part of the very texture of Deguy's poems. They are not, however, any more than are dreams and the unconscious, the Answer; in fact, for all their intellectual atmosphere, Deguy's poems suggest that, for him, if anything is the answer it is the happy—or distressing— confusing mixture of all the complicated thoughts and points of view that delineate his subjects. This kind of complexity is expressed not by a sustained lyric tone—this is less revelation than questioning—but by a changing surface of tones, and kinds of language. The poem proceeds, verbally as well as thematically, by means of hesitations, interruptions, changes. It stops, it diverges; it often has an air of being unfinished— even, one could say, of having gone nowhere, the way a moment goes nowhere, a moment of perception or sensation with all its intermixture of memories, associations, ideas.

Deguy's poems seem, for the most part, to be suggested, or inspired, not by general themes or by dreams and hallucinations but by certain kinds of quickly passing and quickly caught moments of consciousness. The moments are most often ordinary and unspecial. Their significance is felt but not explained. In "Quadratures/5 P.M.," for example, the soft, cool springtime indoor-outdoor emptiness—with, in the kitchen, the shells being taken off time—is memorable without one's knowing why it was this particular moment that suggested that "the face of things could have been changed."

Deguy of course isn't alone in writing a new, nonsurrealist kind of poetry, though he is an unusual practitioner of it. After World War II, the inspirational force of surrealism seemed just about over. The urgency of recent events—Hitler, the war, the Occupation—probably had something to do with it. Also it is possible that the work begun by Baudelaire and Rimbaud had largely been accomplished. So many brilliant poets had written, so many versions of that magic had been dreamed and expressed. Styles and directions in art don't last forever. Reading Perse and Éluard might inspire mere emulation or might incite young poets to do something new. One can guess what might have seemed wrong, in the 1950s, with that poetry: its leaving out so much, its idealizing, its blurriness, its seeming enclosed, too special, too ecstatic, too sure of its own rhetorical powers. The unconscious, which seemed, and was, such a grand escape from unreality, boredom, and sameness, could end up being a cause of them. In any case, whatever happened, it was true that in the 1950s and 1960s, reading Kant or traveling in South America, for example, could be part of what one wanted to get into a poem. Intellectual details, and also very specifically concrete physical details, became attractive, in the poems of Char, Follain, Guillevic, for example. Words, the nature of words, classes of words, language became a poetic subject also—as in Ponge. There was, too, related to this, a self-consciousness about poetry, a wondering about what it was, if there was anything real about it, if it was worth writing. If poetry wasn't "real," as real as "things," it had no business existing. Some poets renounced poetry. Others were attracted to a sort of poetic minimalism, very few words on mostly blank pages. Deguy seemed to come out of all this undiscouraged, full of energy and ideas, seemingly fascinated by a great variety of experiences—intellectual, emotional, and literary—and liking to get them all into his poems. Rather than choosing one strand, or line, of poetic subject matter and style, as have some of his talented contemporaries (Du Bouchet and Bonnefoy, for example), Deguy seems to me to stay in the center, as if he were unwilling to miss anything, didn't want to give anything up, not any of life or any of the "old privileges" of the poet: being able to rhyme, to tell stories, to write long poems, to mix poetry and prose, to be precise and intellectual, to be ecstatic and lyrical, to write about anything he wants.

He writes about a number of "subjects." That is, his poems begin with a number of different apparent subjects—the most frequent are landscape, woman (unfamiliar, seen in public), woman (known and loved), a place encountered while traveling, a philosophical problem, a text, some aspect of writing poetry. The inspiration is characteristically sudden—a thought coming to mind, a landscape seen for a moment—

Hêtre ou tremble au souffle de femme embrassée[2]

2. Beech or aspen in the breath of a woman embraced

("Quadratures," from which this line is taken, consists of seven short poems, each inspired by the same place at different hours of a day.) These inspirations (or little shocks, or excitements) seem to start the music, which at once becomes involved with, and is composed of, all sorts of experiential and intellectual associations. If the starting subject is a thought, an attempt at definition, as in "Desire"—

> If desire is that which makes one leave all the rest for the utterly different which is so only in that it is not the rest that one prefers however

the thinking is likely to quickly encounter physical details that make one forget, almost or partly, what is being said—

> estrus, prompt puberty of sweaters, cramps of pines in July. . . .

Poems starting with physical details—

> Hold this moment where she sits down
> Moderating the skirt to the right to the left the eyes
> Her legs drifting on the tiles allowing

are complicated by reflection and by other ways of observing—

> The fingers to find themselves again the pronomial body

> On the axis where we—for we *are* on the axis
> Customary sojourn under oblong skies
> Surrounded by earth. . . .

The real subject is where the initial subject has been taken, what the whole poem ends up being, and that seems to be usually, in Deguy's work, an emotional event depicted with intellectual lines. The poems are a sort of "advanced study"— using advanced knowledge and techniques—of momentary states, studies that, as in the poem amusingly titled "Advanced Study" (inspired by a brief stay at Princeton), don't lead to intellectual understanding but to something more immediate and more inclusive, emotionally more the truth. In "Advanced Study" the run to the train station with a woman, with its references to Homeric chariot races, the Annunciation, guillotines, and with its pun on *nom* (*name, noun*) and its bizarre words like *siamoisa* and *comparants* (all suggestive of the intellectual skills of a scholar) leads to the poet's saying not only that it wasn't he who just ran to the station but that he doesn't even know who it was and, finally, that he has "forgotten what is (going) to begin." He questions his identity and is confused about time. This far-from-clear conclusion of course makes sense artistically and emotionally. These are just the effects a sudden, unexpected intimacy is likely to have.

Deguy writes in a variety of poetic forms, which include various kinds of "prose poems"—the concentrated intellectual prose of "Desire," the broken-up-into-segments prose of "Etc." In this prose poetry there is a characteristic mixture of plain talk, intellectual talk, poetical talk, excited exclamations, and expressions of feeling. Deguy's prose—

> A toast by Cassiopeia herself and Deneb in honor of our last twinklings! The earth in a mantilla of telstars plays Russian roulette, a "call-girl" cassandra on a Concord toward Caracas or Qatar drinks a glass of champagne between the salvos of Orion and Boötes—

is sometimes more "poetic" (in the sense of extravagant and fanciful) than his verse—

> Vous serez étonnées d'entendre la liberté de Paul
> Corinthiens II. . . .

The verse poems are of various lengths. None rhymes in a regular way, though rhyme, like other poetic devices, may every once in a while appear, at the ends of lines—

> Remonte vers l'actrice de nuit cernée Véga
> Comme Yvette Guilbert ou les cils d'un Degas[3]

---

3. Reascends toward the night actress eye-ringed Vega
   Like Yvette Guilbert or the eyelashes of a Degas

or elsewhere—

> N'gao sud-ouest où dorment les maîtresses. . . .

Line lengths may be similar or varied; sometimes there are stanzas.

There is, in many of the verse poems, a particular, delicate kind of music that comes less from rhymes, stanzas, and line lengths than from syntax and sense, a music of hesitation, of interruption, of sudden silence. This music seems the result of the lines not being finished, logically or grammatically, and of one line not following the line before it. Often the sense of a line is picked up by the next, but not where the other line left it—from someplace else. Sometimes a line, such as the one about petrels and gannets in "This lady and her beautiful window," is as if abandoned or afloat in the middle of a poem to which it seemingly has no connection. The distance between one line and another may be great, as in this case, or it may be small. In any event, one can't read the poem straight through, as one utterance, in one breath, but must keep pausing. The similarity, or harmony, of sounds from one line to the next, however, draws one on—

> Sa beauté la surface
> L'idolâtrie de nos regards croisés
> Mais de plus près la sueur de son nom perle
> Pourtant "quelle heure est-il"
> Alors j'adopte ses caries
> Plus près plus près
> Le visage s'enfuit en rasant ses terres[4]

One can't say if the prosody creates the content or the content the prosody; probably something of both. The hesitation, the

---

4. Her beauty the surface
   The idolatry of our crossed gazes
   But closer the sweat of her name beads
   Nevertheless "what time is it"
   Then I adopt her cavities
   Closer   closer
   My face takes off razing her lands

blanks, the slight vagueness indicate the distance from which, and the kind of space in which, the feeling is taking place.

The formal variety of Deguy's poetry (prose poems, verse poems, great variety of both) seems part of his concern with, his fascination with, the nature of poetry. If poetry's relation to the rest of reality is a problem, the solution to it is at least as much in how, as in what, one writes—different forms are different answers, different views of the problem. Poetry and the poet are also subjects he writes about directly. Letting his concern with poetry (what it is, how to make it, what is its purpose) show in his poems is part of their general openness and inclusiveness, of their tendency to let in and deal with everything that is there.

I have been writing about Deguy's poems as if they were more of a unity than in fact they are. They were written over a period of almost thirty years, and naturally there are changes. A reader going through this book chronologically will see them. Some of the main changes in the verse poems can be seen in reading, say, "The Gulf" and the poem beginning "This lady and her beautiful window." The early, rather Perse-like "The Gulf" is less "intellectual," more openly personal and lyrical, and has a continuing rather than a hesitating, interrupted kind of music. It doesn't change in point of view. It expresses two main feelings—an ecstatic sort of oneness with nature—

> I live at the level of shrill grasshopper bursts.
> And among paper insects scattered by the wind.

and a feeling of difference from nature and of separation from it—

> Everything in me responds to the wind—except . . .
> . . . the voice astonished at its dissimilarity!

Its narrative line is chronological, and it follows its subject to the end. In "This lady and her beautiful window," published six years later (in *Ouï dire*), the hesitating, interrupted music has appeared—

> Cette dame et sa belle fenêtre
> Un ange asymétrique aux ailes porte-vent

There is more variation of tone—

> disait je vous salue
> L'amour distinguait l'absence et la mort

There is language used in a more complicated way—

> Que béatrice soit aussi celle sur qui le temps
> touche un cheveu[5]

(*béatrice* having the sense of *blessèd—béate*—and *Beatrice*—Dante's). There are reversals of roles and ambiguity of pronouns (the angel greets Mary; the poet discovers the woman, but it is she who gives him *salut*—greetings, salvation); more daring transitions, greater spaces between things—as in the leap to the last line. Or one could call this last, and much else that is in the poem, change of perspective. The feeling here in regard to nature is not separation, as in "The Gulf," but oneness, at least for a moment, a feeling of union won out of chaos (mélée) by means of love. The poet and his real (imaginary—idealized) woman are one, in their moment of meeting, with the Angel and Mary in theirs. Each moment is full of the future (a child) and of each future it takes a long time to recognize the meaning. Each of these moments is like the sweet slow meeting of two rivers, the Loire and the Loir (one feminine and one masculine).

The later poem is more sophisticated and intellectual than "The Gulf" but at the same time quite lyric and serene. The complicatedness, the changes of perspective, and the interrupted, hesitating music seem to have helped create a new and interesting artistic balance. In some poems after *Ouï dire*

---

5. This lady and her beautiful window
   An asymmetrical angel with wind-bearing wings
   was saying I greet you
   Love distinguished absence and death
   May Beatrice also be the one time touches a hair of

(especially in *Donnant Donnant*), there is somewhat more crowdedness, rush, and momentary intensity, with a correspondingly slightly rough, hurried music (a kind of texture that earlier appeared more often in his prose poems)—

> Fais comme si tu m'aimais Montre toi montre moi
> Tes Dombes ton Rhine tes Seine ton Ombrie[6]

and, in some poems, published in periodicals since then, a particularly tough sort of intensity applied to physical depiction—

> s'encadre sur la porte verte rajustant blonde
> a l'électricité la tresse l'onde
> et d'une manche glabre de pull
> tire sur la jupe au niveau de l'iliaque

Certain characteristics persist, with variations, in Deguy's poetry. There is crowding and hurry, a feeling of richness and rush in the early poems—

> Orienter insistant courber repassant diriger rassembler
> dans son souffle incliner joindre[7]

though of a simpler kind than, say, in such poems as "Etc.," "Sleeping Under the Star 'N'," "Quadratures," or "I Call Muse"—

> Ting tint Orée Auray tent forest stentor Aretino Parrot
> Tyndareus Paindoré Tintoretto
>
> ("I Call Muse")

vessel that collects urine, oval lucarne of the sky, double-quick umbrella where the neckties unfold, the male fan, the obscene postcards born to the sleeve, the map on the table over which the masters stoop, the antidosis over the grant holder pit, toris exchanged on ring fingers, pink vestiges from hats. . . .

> ("Quadratures")

---

6. Act as if you loved me Show yourself show me
   Your Dombes your Rhine your Seine your Umbria
7. To orient insistent to curve coming back lead gather in its
   blowing to bend to join

There is a direct, expressive tone—in the late poems likely to be more complicated and allusive—that persists, too—

> The cries of a gull my kisses
> That swoop onto the silence of your cheek
>
> ("She," in
> *Fragment du cadastre*)

> I cannot even without your backbone without your antenna
> Tell the time without the clepsydra of your blood
>
> ("Iaculatio Tardiva,"
> in *Donnant Donnant*)

Always present in Deguy's work are his wit, his experimentation, his sensuous intellectuality, the seeming urgency of what he has to say about what moves him to write.

Deguy, though in some of his work he shares a certain adventurous disjunctiveness with some modern American poets, seems to me more fundamentally lyrical and intent on his own experiences, say, than Pound; more attached to "making sense" than John Ashbery; and in general very attached to the French tradition he is continuing and changing. Writers who seem to have influenced him include, for the early work, Éluard and Perse, and for the later, Mallarmé and Jouve.

Poetry is hard to translate. Deguy's, which, like Mallarmé's, for example, is very much embedded in French words and usages, is especially so. Clayton Eshleman, I think, has done exactly the right thing in aiming to be completely accurate and at the same time to give the reader an experience in English equivalent to what he'd have reading Deguy in French.

On the Poetry of Joseph Ceravolo

Modern poetry takes a large step in this poetry that has not yet really been followed by others. It is as if one could see the print of that step in the snow, and then a great beautiful snowy wilderness but no more tracks. In this respect it resembles the work of such poets as John Wheelwright or Gerard Manley Hopkins, its stylistic innovations so bound up with the expression of a particular sensibility as to be, even though inspiring, inimitable.

Ceravolo's poetic subject is often a moment, caught, as it were, off guard and open to all kinds of other moments and their sensations:

> Then there is nothing   think!
> the angular explanation
> boom!   he was a parade
>   with a gift
> a question cable of
>   thought
> a thermos savage in
>   the hotel
> in vera cruz color
>   sand the boat

This is not "just language" (no such remarkable description as that of a man as "a parade with a gift" could be that), but descriptive language arranged and disarranged in such a way as to keep the feelings and ideas fixed in it, fresh and sharp, every time the passage is read. What these lines say, in a prose

---

From Joseph Ceravolo *The Green Lake Is Awake* (Coffeehouse Press, 1994).

way, doesn't make sense in an ordinary way—a human being is not (not without further explanation, in any case) a parade, a cable, or a thermos savage. But what the lines suggest (which is what they say if you take them on what might be termed "poetic faith") makes sense of a kind that is found only in poetry. Another example of a Ceravolo "moment," from this same poem ("Water: How Weather Feels the Cotton Hotels") has a more concentrated, almost microscopic intensity, while at the same time seeming quite large and open:

> earthenware
> drawing its own
> tonight on some
> particular wasp

I knew Joseph Ceravolo and his poems for twenty-five years. He would send me a poem like "How Weather Feels the Cotton Hotels," and, every time, I'd gasp. It was wonderful and I didn't know how he had done it. It faded like the mirage of a gorgeous building; then, as soon as I reread it, it was there again. What was Ceravolo doing? Whatever it was, somehow in four lines he brought me intense, clear feelings of wasps on earthenware, of nights, of feelings wasps must have, that clay pots might have. A new—or, rather, old but unlighted—part of my experience was given light. His poems were a sort of amazing perceptual archaeology.

Rather than explaining ("Seeing this wasp landing . . . ") or conventional poeticizing ("O wasp alighting!"), which risks making such moments banal or false, Ceravolo's method uses indirection, rapid transitions, dissociation, and other kinds of apparent "nonsense." These oddnesses are there not to be resolved but to be given in to, so that the poem can have its say. If one can do that, it's certainly worth it.

There are, in this poetry pairs of seemingly unconnected words—"rice Spring," "Sail glooms," "boom autumn"; and seemingly unconnected phrases and lines—"As far as I look we are across A / boat crosses by. There is no monkey in me / left: Sleep." There are many odd usages, words put together in "incorrect" ways—"These are my clothes to a / boat"—and syntactically unfinished statements:

> Hold me
> Till only,   these are my
>   clothes   I sit.

These oddnesses take place in a context of simplicity, quietness, and directness. They aren't avant-garde explosions for their own sake, but occur when they are necessary to the difficult, exciting expression of whatever has to be said.

> There's nothing to love in this
> rice Spring.
> Collected something warm like friends.
> Sail glooms are none . . .

One could sing this. One would know well enough what it meant.

Ceravolo was influenced by William Carlos Williams; though characteristically his poetry goes elsewhere. In the work of both there is a blurring expansion of identity, a sort of giving oneself completely to a tree, an insect, flowers. Williams's aim, in such poems as "Daisy," "Queen Anne's Lace," and "The Young Sycamore," is usually accomplished in his merging with the thing observed so as to describe it more convincingly. Ceravolo has a tendency to go back and forth from one identity to another:

> I am a dirty little bug
> Plants!, because
> I'm small   because there's no courage
> in me   will you come home
> with me? And
> stay   With us on the bed

When Ceravolo, like Williams, is merely looking, he can be trusted to say what is right there, in the simplest, most direct manner—"man walking with his / shoulders haunched and tufts / of white duck hair in the back / of the head!"; when he goes beyond ordinary perceptions, this atmosphere of accuracy stays with him. It is a quality rare among poets, a combination of clear down-to-earthness with the sort of wild dreaminess of Lorca or Rimbaud, as in this passage from "May":

Morning oh May flower! oh
May exist. Built.
When will water stop
Cooling? Built, falling. Reeds. I am surprised . . .

After the excited, ambiguous invocation (of May), a number of profound ideas are suggested with surprising simplicity and speed: the notion that the month of May has been "Built"; the wondering if water will keep its qualities; the realization that water also has been built, and built, probably, so as to be falling (even falling things are built). After this there is a return to plain physical presence, a fact ("reeds") and plain everyday consciousness ("I am surprised"). Ceravolo's work is full of pleasures like these. Sometimes his sensations are expressed in language that seems as physical as the things he is talking about:

Oak oak! like like
it then
    cold some wild paddle
so sky then . . .

Even the most simply descriptive poems about something seen have a characteristic lift:

The fish are staying here
and eating. The plant is
thin and has very long leaves
like insects' legs, the way
they bend down.
Through the water
the plant breaks from the water:

the line of the water and the air.
Told!

The slowed-down, superimposed perceptions of lines 6, 7, and 8 are extraordinary and all Ceravolo's own.

To read these poems is to be refreshed and surprised. They are the real thing. Their audience may always be limited by one of their great qualities: they are aesthetically uncompromising, and make no gestures or appeals outside themselves. Anyone lucky enough to read them, however, will have one of the great true experiences of twentieth-century poetry.

Presenting John Ashbery
(East Hampton, July 1992)

It is and isn't easy to introduce my old friend John Ashbery. His success is what makes it hard; his work is what makes it easy. Or vice versa. In any case, here he is. He is here, and he has written so many books. He has written a lot of marvelous poems. These poems have changed from book to book; some things about them have stayed the same. I will tell the story of my knowing John and his work, and then I will try to say something that may make his poetry—which is and isn't easy—easier perhaps to get something from when you are hearing him read it.

I met John at Harvard long ago. We were both undergraduates, both poets, and we both ended up being editors of the literary magazine, the *Harvard Advocate*. John's poetry was sweet, mysterious, overwhelming, and convincing, when he was nineteen years old:

> These are amazing: each
> Joining a neighbor, as though speech
> Were a still performance . . .

and

> the fumes are not of a singular authority
> And indeed are dry as poverty

Not published

Maybe he wrote these last two lines when he was a little older than nineteen. In any case, Where, I wondered, did their high authority, that rare refined air they breathed, come from? This was poetry from heights I hadn't seen. John continued to write these kinds of lines, and many variations; by the time he was forty he had a poetic language that seemed capable of beautifully covering everything, like an endlessly incoming transparent tide. I kept wondering at it and being excited by it and never did find out where it came from, except that there was no doubt that it was my sad, witty, brilliant, silly friend John Ashbery who was writing it. What a treat (despite the pains) it has been to know him so long—it's like the luck of being born in Paris (if you like Paris).

This biographical part leaves out almost everything. But it's time to say a few things about his poetry. These things may be right or wrong, it being the nature of poetry as we conceive it that no one, including the poet, can ever say anything about it that is sufficient. Some critics avail themselves generously of this situation by scarcely looking at the poetry at all.

John's poetry is extremely inventive. Technically I think he may be more inventive than Auden, who left hardly any form unturned. Like elephants breaking all the branches, John's poetic progress has left the poetic savanna behind it littered with the ruins of sonnets, sestinas, haiku, prose poems, doggerel, whatever. This wonderful and refreshing technical variety has as its object, I think, an endless attack on the perhaps nonexistent *subject,* the mystery that will never be revealed. Then why keep trying? One keeps trying because it is such a pleasure, such a joy, and in any case for John apparently a necessity. Unhappy though the burden of the song sometimes is, in the writing of it he seems some sort of (if you can imagine it) happy Sisyphus. Get up, fall down, get up, fall down, and the poems keep appearing, full of the conviction (and this seems especially so in his rather astounding long—200 page—poem *Flow Chart*) that this struggle, this poetry of trying to find out, is the great thing to do. I get the idea, in *Flow Chart,* that by now—or by then, for nothing lasts long in John's poetry (I mean, no idea)—in *Flow Chart* I have the impression that John's poetry has arrived at the point where it itself may be the answer. This endless coming and going, hope and deception, impressions of richness and then nothing of the sort, but a new entrance and maybe it is all there again— this is the experience and the texture (an enchanting and alluring one) of being alive.

This of course is exciting and reassuring to a reader. It is alright to be unfocused, easy to distract, confused. There's no penalty for not thinking things through to the end. In fact, it's the contrary. The brilliant diaphonous distractions and asides of the Ashberyan lute may be the only way to find the truth.

To make clarity out of confusion and, just as beautifully, the opposite, John's poetry has the following characteristics:

1) it has a great mixture of tones: the noble, the literary, and the colloquial bump in it together:
> Full many a flower
> is born to blush unseen, and waste its fragrance on the arctic air
> outside the Shady Octopus Saloon, and then some.

2) as is evident in the preceding quotation, it is funny.

3) it combines this funniness (which ranges from the brilliantly witty to the silly) with a seriousness that's sometimes close to the sublime:
> The academy of the future is opening its doors . . .

4) it mingles the positive and the negative inside a single phrase in such a way as to bewilder one back to something probably truer than either:
> Here there is nowhere near the expansive atmosphere we
> imagine we miss

or
> the chorus picks up on hope
> in the black promise facing us. . . .

So these kinds of mix-ups are things you will probably hear in the poems. There may also be a mixture of false and true autobiography, false and true history, isolated details of stories and of history, appearing from nowhere and for no apparent reason—
> Soon all the animals acclaimed the victor. . . .

or
> So seven years passed. . . .

The speed, and with it, the obvious relevance of what seems irrelevant—these are great qualities of John's work. And the occasional craziness I like especially, that is so strong it seems almost to threaten to crack open the whole argument:

> There is nothing like the old beach. The old tables.
> Once, an avalanche of cuties threatened our meeting. Fred
>   bypassed it.

I guess one way to account for it is that by including every-thing (all styles and tones, all degrees of true and false) the poetry gets a strange atmosphere of total control. It gives no quick (false) solutions; it's pervasive; nothing can escape. The writing has to go like blazes to keep up with such a project:

>   it might be that
> No real relation exists between my wish for you
> To return and the movements of your arms and legs.
> But my inability to accept this fact
> Annihilates it. Thus
> My power over you is absolute
> You exist only in me and on account of me—

Reading Ashbery's poems, we, also, may be masters of everything, even though everything is falling to pieces. That seems, while we are reading, to be the state things are in and the best way to be happy with them—after we stop reading, too. For this great gift, we're indebted, alone among his peers, I think, to John Ashbery.

Fresh Air

I

At the Poem Society a black-haired man stands up to say
"You make me sick with all your talk about restraint and
    mature talent!
Haven't you ever looked out the window at a painting by
    Matisse,
Or did you always stay in hotels where there were too many
    spiders crawling on your visages?
Did you ever glance inside a bottle of sparkling pop,
Or see a citizen split in two by the lightning?
I am afraid you have never smiled at the hibernation
Of bear cubs except that you saw in it some deep relation
To human suffering and wishes, oh what a bunch of
    crackpots!"
The black-haired man sits down, and the others shoot arrows
    at him.
A blond man stands up and says,
"He is right! Why should we be organized to defend the
    kingdom
Of dullness? There are so many slimy people connected with
    poetry,
Too, and people who know nothing about it!
I am not recommending that poets like each other and
    organize to fight them,
But simply that lightning should strike them."
Then the assembled mediocrities shot arrows at the blond-
    haired man.
The chairman stood up on the platform, oh he was
    physically ugly!

From *Thank You* (Grove Press, 1962).

He was small-limbed and -boned and thought he was quite
    seductive,
But he was bald with certain hideous black hairs,
And his voice had the sound of water leaving a vaseline
    bathtub,
And he said, "The subject for this evening's discussion is
    poetry
On the subject of love between swans." And everyone threw
    candy hearts
At the disgusting man, and they stuck to his bib and tucker,
And he danced up and down on the platform in terrific
    glee
And recited the poetry of his little friends—but the blond
    man stuck his head
Out of a cloud and recited poems about the east and
    thunder,
And the black-haired man moved through the stratosphere
    chanting
Poems of the relationships between terrific prehistoric
    charcoal whales,
And the slimy man with candy hearts sticking all over him
Wilted away like a cigarette paper on which the bumblebees
    have urinated,
And all the professors left the room to go back to their duty,
And all that were left in the room were five or six poets
And together they sang the new poem of the twentieth
    century
Which, though influenced by Mallarmé, Shelley, Byron, and
    Whitman,
Plus a million other poets, is still entirely original
And is so exciting that it cannot be here repeated.
You must go to the Poem Society and wait for it to
    happen.
Once you have heard this poem you will not love any
    other,
Once you have dreamed this dream you will be
    inconsolable,
Once you have loved this dream you will be as one dead,
Once you have visited the passages of this time's great art!

2

"Oh to be seventeen years old
Once again," sang the red-haired man, "and not know that
poetry
Is ruled with the sceptre of the dumb, the deaf, and the
creepy!"
And the shouting persons battered his immortal body with
stones
And threw his primitive comedy into the sea
From which it sang forth poems irrevocably blue.

Who are the great poets of our time, and what are their
names?
Yeats of the baleful influence, Auden of the baleful
influence, Eliot of the baleful influence
(Is Eliot a great poet? no one knows), Hardy, Stevens,
Williams (is Hardy of our time?),
Hopkins (is Hopkins of our time?), Rilke (is Rilke of our
time?), Lorca (is Lorca of our time?), who is still of our
time?
Mallarmé, Valéry, Apollinaire, Éluard, Reverdy, French
poets are still of our time,
Pasternak and Mayakovsky, is Jouve of our time?

Where are young poets in America, they are trembling in
publishing houses and universities,
Above all they are trembling in universities, they are bathing
the library steps with their spit,
They are gargling out innocuous (to whom?) poems about
maple trees and their children,
Sometimes they brave a subject like the Villa d'Este or a
lighthouse in Rhode Island,
Oh what worms they are! They wish to perfect their
form.

Yet could not these young men, put in another profession,
Succeed admirably, say at sailing a ship? I do not doubt it,
Sir, and I wish we could try them.
(A plane flies over the ship holding a bomb but perhaps it
will not drop the bomb,

The young poets from the universities are staring anxiously
    at the skies,
Oh they are remembering their days on the campus when
    they looked up to watch birds excrete,
They are remembering the days they spent making their
    elegant poems.)

Is there no voice to cry out from the wind and say what it is
    like to be the wind,
To be roughed up by the trees and to bring music from the
    scattered houses
And the stones, and to be in such intimate relationship with
    the sea
That you cannot understand it? Is there no one who feels
    like a pair of pants?

3

Summer in the trees! "It is time to strangle several bad
    poets."
The yellow hobbyhorse rocks to and fro, and from the
    chimney
Drops the Strangler! The white and pink roses are slightly
    agitated by the struggle,
But afterwards beside the dead "poet" they cuddle up
    comfortingly against their vase. They are safer now, no
    one will compare them to the sea.

Here on the railroad train, one more time, is the Strangler.
He is going to get that one there, who is on his way to a
    poetry reading.
Agh! Biff! A body falls to the moving floor.

In the football stadium I also see him,
He leaps through the frosty air at the maker of comparisons
Between football and life and silently, silently strangles him!

Here is the Strangler dressed in a cowboy suit
Leaping from his horse to annihilate the students of myth!

The Strangler's ear is alert for the names of Orpheus,
Cuchulain, Gawain, and Odysseus,

And for poems addressed to Jane Austen, F. Scott
  Fitzgerald,
To Ezra Pound, and to personages no longer living
Even in anyone's thoughts—O Strangler the Strangler!

He lies on his back in the waves of the Pacific Ocean.

4

Supposing that one walks out into the air
On a fresh spring day and has the misfortune
To encounter an article on modern poetry
In *New World Writing*, or has the misfortune
To see some examples of some of the poetry
Written by the men with their eyes on the myth
And the Missus and the midterms, in the *Hudson Review*,
Or, if one is abroad, in *Botteghe Oscure*,
Or indeed in *Encounter*, what is one to do
With the rest of one's day that lies blasted to ruins
All bluely about one, what is one to do?
Oh surely one cannot complain to the President,
Nor even to the deans of Columbia College,
Nor to T. S. Eliot, nor to Ezra Pound,
And supposing one writes to the Princess Caetani,
"Your poets are awful!" what good would it do?
And supposing one goes to the *Hudson Review*
With a package of matches and sets fire to the building?
One ends up in prison with trial subscriptions
To the *Partisan, Sewanee,* and *Kenyon Review!*

5

Sun out! perhaps there is a reason for the lack of poetry
In these ill-contented souls, perhaps they need air!

Blue air, fresh air, come in, I welcome you, you are an art
  student,
Take off your cap and gown and sit down on the chair.
Together we shall paint the poets—but no, air! perhaps you
  should go to them, quickly,
Give them a little inspiration, they need it, perhaps they are
  out of breath,

Give them a little inhuman company before they freeze the
   English language to death!
(And rust their typewriters a little, be sea air! be noxious! kill
   them, if you must, but stop their poetry!
I remember I saw you dancing on the surf on the Côte
   d'Azur,
And I stopped, taking my hat off, but you did not remember
   me,
Then afterwards you came to my room bearing a handful of
   orange flowers
And we were together all through the summer night!)

That we might go away together, it is so beautiful on the sea,
   there are a few white clouds in the sky!

But no, air! you must go . . . Ah, stay!

But she has departed and . . . Ugh! what poisonous fumes
   and clouds! what a suffocating atmosphere!
Cough! whose are these hideous faces I see, what is this
   rigor
Infecting the mind? where are the green Azores,
Fond memories of childhood, and the pleasant orange
   trolleys,
A girl's face, red-white, and her breasts and calves, blue eyes,
   brown eyes, green eyes, fahrenheit
Temperatures, dandelions, and trains, O blue?!
Wind, wind, what is happening? Wind! I can't see any bird
   but the gull, and I feel it should symbolize . . .
Oh, pardon me, there's a swan, one two three swans, a great
   white swan, hahaha how pretty they are! Smack!
Oh! stop! help! yes, I see—disrespect for my superiors—
   forgive me, dear Zeus, nice Zeus, parabolic bird, O
   feathered excellence! white!
There is Achilles too, and there's Ulysses, I've always wanted
   to see them,
And there is Helen of Troy, I suppose she is Zeus too, she's
   so terribly pretty—hello, Zeus, my you are beautiful,
   Bang!

One more mistake and I get thrown out of the Modern
   Poetry Association, help! Why aren't there any adjectives
   around?
Oh there are, there's practically nothing else—look, here's
   *grey, utter, agonized, total, phenomenal, gracile, invidious,
   sundered,* and *fused,*
Elegant, absolute, pyramidal, and . . . Scream! but what can I
   describe with these words? States!
States symbolized and divided by two, complex states, magic
   states, states of consciousness governed by an aroused
   sincerity, cockadoodle doo!
Another bird! is it morning? Help! where am I? am I in the
   barnyard? oink oink, scratch, moo! Splash!
My first lesson. "Look around you. What do you think and
   feel?" *Uhhh* . . . "Quickly!" *This Connecticut landscape would
   have pleased Vermeer.* Wham! A-Plus. "Congratulations!" I
   am promoted.
OOOhhhhh I wish I were dead, what a headache! My
   second lesson: "Rewrite your first lesson line six hundred
   times. Try to make it into a magnetic field." I can do it
   too. But my poor line! What a nightmare! Here comes a
   tremendous horse.
Trojan, I presume. No, it's my third lesson. "Look, look!
   Watch him, see what he's doing? That's what we want you
   to do. Of course it won't be the same as his at first, but . . . "
   I demur. Is there no other way to fertilize minds?
Bang! I give in . . . Already I see my name in two or three
   anthologies, a serving girl comes into the barn bringing
   me the anthologies,
She is very pretty and I smile at her a little sadly, perhaps it
   is my last smile! Perhaps she will hit me! But no, she
   smiles in return, and she takes my hand.
My hand, my hand! what is this strange thing I feel in my
   hand, on my arm, on my chest, my face—can it be . . . ? it
   is! AIR!
Air, air, you've come back! Did you have any success? "What
   do you think?" I don't know, air. You are so strong,
   air.

And she breaks my chains of straw, and we walk down the
  road, behind us the hideous fumes!
Soon we reach the seaside, she is a young art student who
  places her head on my shoulder,
I kiss her warm red lips, and here is the Strangler, reading
  the *Kenyon Review!* Good luck to you, Strangler!
Goodbye, Helen! goodbye, fumes! goodbye, abstracted
  dried-up boys! goodbye, dead trees! goodbye, skunks!
Goodbye, manure! goodbye, critical manicure! goodbye, you
  big fat men standing on the east coast as well as the west
  giving poems the test! farewell, Valéry's stern dictum!
Until tomorrow, then, scum floating on the surface of
  poetry! goodbye for a moment, refuse that happens to
  land in poetry's boundaries! adieu, stale eggs teaching
  imbeciles poetry to bolster up your egos! adios, boring
  anomalies of these same stale eggs!
Ah, but the scum is deep! Come, let me help you! and soon
  we pass into the clear blue water. Oh GOODBYE, castrati
  of poetry! farewell, stale pale skunky pentameters (the
  only honest English meter, gloop gloop!)! until tomorrow,
  horrors! oh, farewell!

Hello, sea! good morning, sea! hello, clarity and excitement,
  you great expanse of green—

O green, beneath which all of them shall drown!

II

Some South American Poets

Jorge Guinhieme (1887–)

Boiling Water

The boiling water, Father, and princely teacher
Whose first reckoning with boiling water
The teeth of the far center will vindicate for seeds
Of us who have lost the first battle!
That boiling water is the dream
Of Jorge Guiells of the Civil Guard—
Every night he washes his passion in it,
Hoping that it will not rub off on the white ribs of Sevilla.
His mother watches him. With five ribs for screen
The dusty night darkens what he has willed.

Cabaña Ailanthus

At the Cabaña Ailanthus when night breezes are stilled
One old commonwealth teacher remains fastened to his desk.
Through the night come the sounds of the frog
As if someone, or as if an entire people, had learned a
    Romance language.

From *The Pleasures of Peace* (Grove Press, 1969).

Obscurity

When the dark night obscures of our tiny village the immense
　　and topless steeple
Then we heard the bells ring out, for fear that some men
　　might entrance not gain
To their preferred Eastern lights. But a fountain of
　　anachronistic feathers
Darkens the blood of the priest gown before speechlessly he
　　utter the ungracious words.

From The Streets of Buenos Aires

Roseway

O unfeigned laughter of a fine young girl—
Or even of one not so fine—
Young girl, that is the essential thing,
And laugh unfeigned—
But how can you not be fine beneath your roses?

Cabaña de Turistas, Calle de Suenos (Dreams)

Here, where there are tourists
Gathered, let us carry
From one of them to another
The money from their country
That they may see
We do not wish it for ourselves
But only that they may share with one another
What they have.

Pleasure Street

When all are sleeping
The staccato of those not sleeping
Is a mysterious graph on which
The mathematics teacher studies nightly
To find the stars.

Calle Rosa

Roseway, oh lovely girl,
Your face is like a tulip.

I have tulip[1] too, my lovely girl,
And happily will mingle them with yours.

Met-You Street

More open to the light
Than many little streets
This one on which I met you
Carrying a basket of light
To the sea, is my preferred one of
All the little by-ways of the city.

Luis de Calliens (1918–)

Cancion de Noche

A catacomb of feathers
Boiling. A frame.
The steep frame of ducks' loves roiling
Together the fantastic pathways.

Now a drumstick of night,
Two Indians on a highway—
One stricter than a feather,
The other, clasped by might.

To a Dream

Chuckle out, great planned song
Of the ages!
Laugh ages henceforth to be so free!
We are the ones who knew you in
Your star-spangled babyhood—
We are the perusers of your eternal rose!

The Morgan Library

I, Luis de Calliens, Spanish teacher
And South American poet, as I am known,
See now in Nueva York this Morgan Library
Spattered by the mutual funds of her bloody night.

---

1. "Tulip" is in English in the original—*Trans.*

The rich in Nueña de Cangias do not build libraries
And the poor carry a network of berries into the future's
   light.

Luis Cariges (1922–)

Peripher-Argentine

How many stories, bought from love and rain,
This testimony winks to see. Above
These Herculean heights,
Peripher-Argentine,
And far above the desecrated woodlands
And the hopeless farmlands
And the testimonials of bright Western night
A human voice begins a styptic melody
Corroded by your blossoms
Indifferent to the month
And year of every star—
O Argentine!

Besos

My mouth, a cascade of kisses!
And, purely below me, your mouth too,
An equal cascade of remembrance, farms of bliss,
Evidence, preoccupation, evening stars,
Truly, reversing our tables,
When, at dusk, we reform
Trees to their original grandeur,
As nude as each other's stars.

Music

A song creates its own music.

Juan Garcia (1940–)

Plaint

O rolling mountains of my native fascist unconscious mother!
O divine transcendence of some future impassioned stream!

When the souls of the billionaires shall lie streaming in the
   bloodied
Banknotes of a whorish fantasma, whose plucked grace notes
   the hideous transactor no longer
Imbues with the maleficent horror of death's magnificent
   scream!

What, O rolling native mountains whose fascist resistances
Strike against the mutinied hearts of mothers, of orphans, of
   knees
Of silence, what are your invocations, to me, and to my
   mother poets,
What emblems do you carry for us? when shall we strike the
   DOLLARO from the hideous mustang of our homes?

Ode to Guinhieme

When shall we strike the dollaro, magnificent poet, betrayer
   of your class?
When shall we tear the mould-headed thread-ribbed dollaro
   to pieces?
Speak, Guinhieme, if you know . . . but you do not know, and
   you will not speak. You spew wildly into your lunch!

Vactha (193?–)

Campanho

Roll, little garden fields, away!
No longer the garden, they insist
As proper for a muse. This time, however, once peruse
The mist and that fair fountain
Which is reflected there
As in the early starlight
Over Buenos Aires
It begins to rain.
First drops!

Torcito

Brilliant little baby, walk
Across the portico. There, a smiling mama
Will take you in her arms. You will smile.

And I too shall smile. And in this poem I shall enshrine you
   forever!

The *Hasos* in Argentine Poetry

The essence of Argentinian poetry is the *hasos,* or fallen limb.
I do not know if my English readers will get a clear idea of this
structural element of poetry without some further words of
explanation. *Hasosismo,* or the "art of the fallen limb," a tech-
nique which was buried deep in the history and classicism of
the poetry of our Argentine, is recently brought into the fore-
ground by works of masters who have seen what long was
hidden, that to be authentically new the poet is obliged to find
poetic elements which are authentically old—that is, authenti-
cally *his own.* For we do not exist in the new, but in the
permanent—where all is both old and new—and it is the
poet's task precisely to remind us of this condition. The "art of
the fallen limb," insofar as it can be separated from the Ar-
gentinisms of prosodic and syllabic ramifications, may be, I
suppose, briefly said to be *the art of concealing in one line what
has been revealed in the previous line.* Younger practitioners and,
above all, explicators of the *hasosismo* have made often the
error of seeing this function as the reverse of what it actually
is: the revelation in one line of what was concealed in the
preceding—or, the concealing in one line of what is to be
revealed in the next. This is not hasosismo: this is fancy and
the commonest and most ordinary of poetic and all narrative
processuses. HASOSISMO IS THE MYSTERY OF NIGHT
COVERED BY THE DAY; IT IS NOT THE DAY, WHICH
IS REVEALED AFTER BEING HIDDEN IN THE NIGHT.
The difference here is one of heights to plains. San Baz has
hasosismo; Cediz does not. Juanero is a million miles from
having it. In Batorje it is supreme.

Guinhieme*

Hasosismo is difficult to illustrate, since by its very nature it
tends to cover its own tracks. Furthermore, in translation

much is necessarily to be lost, but the attempt is worth making, since this heartstone of poetry deserves to be known beyond our language. Here are some examples from the middle work of Batorje:

> The streets of the city are shining, wet with light
> In the dark and dry forgetfulness of rivers . . .
> > *Motion of Trees* (1932)

> You give me your hand, it is white with pointed
> Forests accepting the horizon . . .
> > *Moon Breed* (1936)

> We stand in clouds. The highest tree, far beneath us
> Our underwater stamina muddies toward her true contempt.
> Indians once walked along this grit with plastic bells
> Whose trees only her final simplicity can chide . . .
> > *Modern* (1943)

In San Baz can be found experiments in using the *hasos* within the line, rather than in succeeding lines. The inspiration from Batorje seems self-evident:

> Sweet dreams! dry daylight sounds without feeling or
> > image—
> > SAN BAZ, *October on the Railroad* (1960)

> I look at you. Oceans of beer gush from the left side of my
> > collar bone.
> > SAN BAZ, *Madam* (1964)

Garcia, in attempting to use the *hasos* politically, has, I think, essentially weakened its poetic function, but some of his examples have a notable strength:

> The Fascists have tied up their mistresses:
> One set of brawny men kicking another in the teeth!
> > JUAN GARCIA, *The Mistresses of Garcia* (1962)

> They have befouled us
> With the perfumes of exultation.
> > JUAN GARCIA, *Homage* (1964)

Calliens, in perhaps too academic a way, has praised the *hasos* in verses using it themselves. Of the long (200 lines) poem, these verses are characteristic:

> A small brain, you are a wide heart;
> A great inspirer, you seek only liquids;
> Sainthood, O Hasos, the bed-land of America!
> A street without silence, you are the steel one;
> My heart without drama, you pet the mammal dog;
> O Hasos, my clear observation!
>
> CALLIENS, *In Praise of Hasos* (1961)

An example of what *hasos* is NOT, though it has sometimes been thought to be:

> A dark congregation of valleys
> Suddenly brings us the sea.
>
> LUIS CEDIZ, *Atalanta* (1943)

From my own work, in conclusion, two examples, one of which I believe to have the *hasos,* the other not:

> The dark pagan of the sea
> Rolls endlessly into our childhood . . .
>
> *Flavinia* (1936)

> Mountains reverberate; seas roar
> For the Christhood in which they believe.
>
> *Otros Cristos* (1957)

J.G.

Reflections On *Hasosismo*

Hasosismo in a pure state mocks the punditism of the masters. Guinhieme's "hasosismo" is no more the pure form that appeared in Lope than is Guilha's "structured license." Neither modern writer has bothered to do his scholarship well. Both have confused a linguistic particularity with a technic structure of design.

Hasosismo, as we encounter it in Lope and in certain of his contemporaries, is no more than a fixed, and academically fixed and predetermined way of avoiding the vulgar and over-explicit in every instance. One characteristic function of this kind of esthetico-literary lèse-majesté is the avoiding of revealed nakedness, a gently clothing over of all that is too barely and openly flung before the reader's eyes.

In Gomero and Pepite this one aspect of true *hasosismo,* which to Guinhieme is *hasosismo* itself and entire, was stressed at the expense of the whole and true concept, which no longer seemed to fit an age of vulgarity and expansion. Gomero's "hasosismo" was the artist's *réplique* to a time which he found too vulgar to share his concerns and certainly his visions. The thing stated was immediately hidden: it is an art of the standstill. We feel the anguish of his time in this technique.

This is not all of *hasosismo.* To Guinhieme and to others of a modern time, a time which feels itself more anguished perhaps than that of a Gomero or a Pepite, this one use of *hasosismo* necessarily appeals. The mistake is forgiven as soon as it is understood. But the term is vulgarized in the process. Of all the foci of Argentine esthetics it is this one (*hasosismo*) which it most imports, perhaps, to retain in purity. For true *hasosismo* has reference to both diction and structure. Without this knowledge the student of Lope is fatally handicapped before he has begun.

Omero Pecad, *Studies for a Leftist University,*
Buenos Aires, 1963.

Homage

A long line of lyricists
Starting with Lope
Move toward the station—
Listen to them shouting!
Look at their breeziness!
They have befouled us
With the perfumes of exultation!

Listen to them praising!
Whom do they praise now?
Francisco Franco!
Demagogues and Popes!

Look at them grazing!
What do they feed on now?
Aspirations, hopes!

Ah let us destroy them
Immediately!
Cut up their breeches!
Turn them into baloney!
Feed them to the pigs, when
Darkness is approaching!
Lyricist! Hash! Over here!

JUAN GARCIA

October on the Railroad

A pure blue sun in the sky! the red leaves fall.
Some of the yellow ones are still holding on to their branches.
And in the distance I hear the engine roar.
October on the railroad! Sometimes, like a rhinoceros,
Fierce and angry, the gray locomotive will come
Tearing the leaf-beds to pieces, and at other times
The engine is gentle, a lakeside hotel
Perhaps, where one's mistress is staying.
One longs to see her—is it a dream?
Sweet dreams! dry daylight sounds without feeling or image
Consult the atlas of a goodbye! And now the train!
Will it take me to Switzerland, do you think? Bavaria?
That depends, O stems, upon your road . . .

GARCIA SAN BAZ

Madame

I look at you. Oceans of beer gush from the left side of my
   collar bone
And down my sides, until they form a crystal pool at my feet
In which children are swimming. I push them back and to
   one side.
Perhaps to love you only it has been given
To me, lady beyond many sorrows. Perhaps you are not of
   the Mistresses of Garcia
Or of Streets Which Are Waving Goodbye. But I love you.
   Straw sailors
Come out of my brow. They coast in that fresh sea sky.

GARCIA SAN BAZ

70

Meadows

Prairies outside dormant cities, America of dreams!
There is no reason for you to be without collarbone.
Without dentistry, yes, they have killed him many times,
But not the definitive movies which showed him rolling
In a pirate flag uphill. No, I am not explaining
Too much. I think you walk quietly to me.
Do you remember what our feeling was
Before we took positions up? Then, quietly walking over
Was all we asked of life. Perhaps the days
Were shorter then, though they are not long now.
Perhaps the only thing we said was Yes
To a dreamy tyrant who has enslaved us now
In the boughs of a tree. The pig raved and slept.
In trains we have been shorter than our pampas.

GARCIA SAN BAZ

71

Homage to Jorge Guinhieme

Jorge Guinhieme, a leading writer and, according to many, founder, of the hasosistic school of Argentine poetry, was born in Buenos Aires in 1887. These tributes to him, along with this selection of his new poems, were originally published in Milagro *(XCVII-4) earlier this year. Guinhieme's volumes include* Byways *(1913),* Hombre *(1930),* Otros Cristos *(1957), and his continuing life work,* The Streets of Buenos Aires.

One may wish to slaughter or to save the bull—but first one must master the cape. With the politics I differ; for the man I feel nothing but love. Without him I might never have been a poet. His esthetic discoveries were powerful enough to enable me to dispute with him to the death in an arena where the combat is eternal: the arena of poetry.

Juan Garcia

My first meeting with Jorge Guinhieme took place in October, 1956. The Argentine springtime was just beginning to cast its argent blossoms—for which the country is named, Guinhieme told me—all about, covering paseo and avenue with a beautiful surface season of their own, when the doorbell I had pushed with such impressment and anxiety on the reddish-blue door at 43 Calle de las piñas, sounded, and, as if by its own command, the door opened to reveal to me a cascade of blossoms, more silver than those on the streets: old, white-haired, laughing Guinhieme, attired in his garments of laughter, warmth, and ease. We soon found that we were in agreement on all the details of poetic diction and structure on which our colloquy

---

From *Paris Review* 47 (1969).

touched. Guinhieme's mind has an amazing freshness, which is one of the facts most memorable of those I carried away from that extraordinary afternoon. And his knowledge of so many matters was astonishing. Guinhieme, salute! And that for which I remember him best is his warmth and friendship, his air of easy welcome to a young man he had no necessity to know, and none whatever to receive.

Fidelio Corazon

I first saw Jorge Guinhieme at the Presidential Gala in 1948. I was introduced to him by a fellow poet—Garcia San Baz. I shall not soon forget my emotion when Guinhieme turned to me and said, "Yes, I have read your poems. You are the speaker of a new generation." But he said more then as well: "Do not forget the achievements of those who have come before. A shallow and tinny contemporaneity is no substitute for the *hasos* of the heart!" It was at the time of Guinhieme's great study of and exposition to us all of the *hasos*. He had no need to speak of "those who have come before," for he was ahead of us then as he is now. His most recent poem, "Flowering Breakfast," is both stylistically and hasosistically an advance on everything that has been done. For fifty years South American poetry has been triumphant: for fifty years it has followed where Guinhieme has led.

Jorge Foxe-Mariño

Great men have their seasons. For Guinhieme it has been perpetually spring. At the age of eighty he continues to write his *Streets of Buenos Aires,* whose subject matter is almost entirely girls! Dear old Guinhieme! Yet we dare not patronize his sensuality because we are younger than he. Not because of piety (true poetry, true poets have no need of that) or of thinking that we too shall some day be old, but quite simply because his poems contain a sensuality, a vivid, a dazzling sexuality, which is nowhere else to be found, neither in art nor

in experience. What can we say? Guinhieme at eighty—a park
filled with blossoming branches.

Reno Guitar

Jorge Guinhieme

From *The Streets of Buenos Aires*

Daffodil Wine

When every street in Buenos Aires
Has at last been enclosed in a poem
I shall get drunk on daffodil wine
And celebrate seventy years of bachelorhood.
O Guinhieme! must you have always wine
When you are already drunk with years?

Watercress Street

A humble street! I see
A girl! She has orange sleeves,
Orange dress, orange shoes!
You belong on Orange Street!
No, I don't! says she.

Ruiz Avenue

Ruiz Avenue you are the heart-line of the city,
Its tempo and pulse, its artery, its medulla oblongata,
And yet you are not my favorite street.
Pushed about on your corners, one feels one has made
An error, that there is something wrong with the whole
    conception of the city.

Calle de las piñas

Oh my own street!
At last, after so many chimneys,
So many barking dogs,
So many fragrant bodies of girls!
My own street! my own chimney!
My own barking dogs! And—who can tell . . . ?

Flowering Breakfast

Flowering breakfast, old secrecy downed with remorse,
You are fearless and speckled, hurt horse of my foreignness
Which sleeps with me on burning ways. It is night, old master
Of ruins, and now it is morning. Flowering breakfast—
Roses, hyacinths, Queen Anne's lace, poppies
Which give sleep, tulips which bring awakening,
Chrysanthemums, each one stuck in this morning's eye
Like an arugula branch. And it is time
For my coffee, old bent stabilities of Chinese fortress
Of winter and failing snow. Guinhieme! arise!
It is late! Your flowering breakfast
Is an invitation to the skies!

From *One Thousand Avant-Garde Plays*

A Song to the Avant-Garde

Tenor:
    In the beginning
    The Avant-Garde
    Was just a silly little thing,
    Coconut-colored sidewalks,
    Women with blue-white parasols
    Tilting over backward
    Or half backward—
    In the beginning—
    And then it grew, and became gigantic and hard
    Like a great, great stone, the Avant-Garde—
    Like a great, great stone that had usurped all of history!

Chorus of Émigré artists in Paris:
    Oh, we'll walk down Apollinaire bis
    Nine ninety nine
    And construct back lugs
    And clunk valentines
    Of paired Z's
    Ha ha ha ha, ha ha, hoo hoo
    Ho Avant-Garde clear and light blue.

Tenor:
    Everything went in fear of it,
    Everyone walked in fear of it—
    And yet it had no power, really,
    It had no lasting power.

From *One Thousand Avant-Garde Plays* (Knopf, 1988).

If now we celebrate it,
It is to salute it and to recognize it,
It is to urge it a little more to take the initiative,
Even though it might, by being so strange,
Destroy us! O Avant-Garde!
Come back, take heart, and tell us now
What life will, and what art will, do!

Ghostly Voice (*offstage*):
Maybe my mission is finished.
Each movement in culture or history is but a stage
Fitting to the age
And it may be the one I had is ended.

Tenor:
Oh say not so, Avant-Garde!
For those of us who have really loved you,
Nothing, no one else can be as hard,
And pure, and true.

Ghostly Voice:
Well, then I'll try to be with you again!

(*Great hullabaloo, wind, musical instruments, sounds of rending, tearing, crackling thunder, as of the Second Coming; and the* AVANT-GARDE *appears—she is a small, old woman.*)

Tenor:
Avant-Garde! What's happened?

Avant-Garde:
This is but the initial phase!

(*She waves a wand or stick, there is a crackle of blue and red lightning, and she is transformed into a shining, almost blinding* CUBE.)

Cube:
ANDIAM!

(CUBE *goes offstage triumphantly.*)

After the Return of the
Avant-Garde

(*Large city square.* MAN *and* WOMAN *standing near a door.*)

Woman:
    They said of the Avant-Garde
    That it had no lasting power
    But now it has come back
    And everything is changed!

Man:
    Yes, look!
    The door has changed
    Through which we used to walk!

Woman:
    It is no longer a door now—
    It is a mosque!

(ARABS *come out of the door, playing saxophones.*)

Man driving past in a car:
    What do you think is the most beautiful thing
    In the Avant-Garde city?

Woman at a window:
    Any three buildings taken alone.

From *One Thousand Avant-Garde Plays* (Knopf, 1988).

Man coming down in a parachute:
   What about the whole of the Avant-Garde city?

Person with feet sticking up out of a manhole:
   That, too, is beautiful, but in a different way.

(*Night falls. Darkness.* ANNOUNCER *speaks from high on a roof with a searchlight.*)

Announcer:
   Which is more avant-garde—a giraffe or an elephant?

Respondent (*from below*):
   A giraffe is more avant-garde, but an elephant is more
      surreal.

(*Music.*)

A Tale of Two Cities

(*Large public square in the Avant-Garde City.*)

Conical Man:
    Our Avant-Garde City is filled with sunlight—
    How beautiful it is!
    No city like this exists in China.

(*Enter* COOK.)

Cook:
    No, certainly not!
    In China our city must be very practical—

(COOK *dances about in a sort of geometrical pattern, as if to show where things are in the Chinese city.*)

    With restaurant available at every five hundred feet—
    That is why Cook work well and have sure of job.
    As for new touristic hotel
    There are going up
    Even if many thing not function properly
    And so—And so here too you see is lumberyard
    And place to change chalk into fire for cook
    And this to talk
    Back and forth telephone, that hardly work. This
    Is our Chinese city.

From *One Thousand Avant-Garde Plays* (Knopf, 1988).

Conical Man:
    And here is our City of the Avant-Garde.
    Not as practical, of course, in a practical kind of way,
    But intensely enjoyable, and suggestive, you'll see,
        Cook—
    And I think you'll like in China, before too long,
    Once you have your practicalities, some like this one too.
    Come, I'll show you around.
    Take this Butterfly Mailbox, for instance,
    That gives wishes! And this time-stopping gasoline
        station
    Whose pumps are dreams! Oh, this, and more—
    Our windows full of cries of alarm and kisses!
    Our sidewalks that explode in thirty flowers
    Of blood! All this, oh everything we give to you,
    Cook, all that you did not need,
    Or did not know you did before!

Cook:
    Now all is evident!
    Avant-Garde will come to China, too,
    If I can get it there.
    I must go home, start work.
    But how to go there!

(*She sees a Dada rocket and looks questioningly at* CONICAL MAN.)

Conical Man:
    Here, take this Dada rocket, Cook. Good luck. Good-bye!

Cook:
    Good-bye.

(COOK *gets on rocket and flies off.*)

Conical Man:
    Oh, it's just another day
    In the Avant-Garde City,
    The only place where such things come to pass—

I'd guess so anyway.
I'm sorry, though, Cook left—
I'd come to like her.

(*He walks off, a little sadly, as an avant-garde concert begins in the public square: musique concrète, featuring saws, vacuum cleaners, firetrucks, and breaking glass.*)

Manet

(Paris, in the nineteenth century.)

Man:
What is the connection

Woman:
Between the newly emerging modern democratic society

Man:
And the art of Edouard Manet?

Woman:
Here. This book tells it.

(Time passes and society is altered: there are the sights and sounds of the twentieth century.)

Both:
And now it has all gone away!

———————

From *One Thousand Avant-Garde Plays* (Knopf, 1988).

Searching for Fairyland

(*Mist.*)

William Butler Yeats:
  I have coom all this distance, lookin for faeryland.

Old Crone:
  Well, ye have time, auld father. Tis not yet dark.

William Butler Yeats:
  Accents change, and all things change, but Beauty is like
    a stone.

(*A snowfall.*)

From *One Thousand Avant-Garde Plays* (Knopf, 1988).

Six *Hamlet* Plays

Smoking Hamlet

Hamlet:
To be, or not to be: that is the question.
Whether 'tis nobler in the mind to suffer
The slings and arrows of outrageous fortune
Or to take arms against a sea of troubles
And by opposing end them.

(HAMLET *lights a cigarette, inhales, exhales, and walks offstage.*)

La Comtesse de Bercy Hamlet

(*Enter, en toute élégance, Anne,* COMTESSE DE BERCY.)

Comtesse:
To be, or not to be: that is the question.
Whether 'tis nobler in the mind to suffer
The slings and arrows of outrageous fortune
Or to take arms against a sea of troubles
And by opposing end them.

(*At the end, a strong wind blows and her clothes swirl all about her.*)

Team Hamlet

(*Six* TEAM MEMBERS *stand in a line facing the audience. Each says, in order, one syllable of Hamlet's "To be, or not to be" speech. After every six syllables, or after every poetic line, the* TEAM MEMBERS *change their posture—they sit, kneel, turn sideways, stand backward, lie down, etc.*)

From *One Thousand Avant-Garde Plays* (Knopf, 1988).

Little Red Riding Hamlet

(LITTLE RED RIDING HOOD's *house; outside it, a forest; then* GRAND-MOTHER's *house. While an offstage* VOICE *recites Hamlet's speech, the story Little Red Riding Hood is acted out in dumb show.*)

Voice:
    To be, or not to be: that is the question.

(LITTLE RED RIDING HOOD's MOTHER *gives her a basket.* LITTLE RED RIDING HOOD *leaves home.*)

Voice:
    Whether 'tis nobler in the mind to suffer

(LITTLE RED RIDING HOOD *encounters the* WOLF.)

Voice:
    The slings and arrows of outrageous fortune

(LITTLE RED RIDING HOOD *walks on to* GRANDMOTHER's *house, goes in and finds the* WOLF *in bed disguised as* GRANDMOTHER, *and questions him.*)

Voice:
    Or to take arms against a sea of troubles

(*The* WOLF *attacks* LITTLE RED RIDING HOOD. *She cries out. The* WOODSMAN *arrives.*)

Voice:
    And by opposing end them.

(*The* WOODSMAN *kills the* WOLF, *splits him open, rescues* GRAND-MOTHER *and all is well.*)

Hamlet Rebus

(A very big, white EGG *is onstage.)*

Hamlet:
   To be, or not to be: that is the question.

*(*CHICKEN *comes out of* EGG, HAMLET *smiles, and continues.)*
   Whether 'tis nobler in the mind to suffer

(Enraged FORTUNE *figure comes on and attacks* HAMLET *and the* CHICKEN *with slung stones and arrows.)*
   The slings and arrows of outrageous fortune

(After slinging and shooting at HAMLET, FORTUNE *disappears.)*
   Or to take arms against a sea of troubles

(Big noise of waves, tempest, crashing, screams and moans. HAMLET *draws his sword.)*
   And by opposing end them.

(He rushes off. The sounds cease.)

Transposed Hamlet

*(*HAMLET, *wearing avant-garde clothes.)*

Hamlet
   Tube heat, or nog tube heat: data's congestion.
   Ladder tricks snow blur Hindu mine dew sulphur
   Tea slinks end harrows have ow! Cages portion
   Orc tube rake harms hay canst a Z oeuf bubbles
   Ant ply cop posy kingdom.

(He goes crazy.)

The Theatre at Epidauros

(*It is very dry and very hot. On the stage of the ancient Greek theater, Greek* ACTORS *are rehearsing lines from tragedies.*)

First Actor:
 The tender body of your first-born son
 Is what you have eaten here—

Second Actor:
 As he died, I was splattered
 By the dark red fountain of his blood,
 And I was happy, as if I were a garden
 Nourished by the fresh spring rain.

Third Actor:
 My brother is dead. Let's stomp on his corpse!

(A LITTLE DOG *runs onstage and nips at the* ACTORS' *heels.*)

Little Dog:
 Argh argh argh argh greeouw!

Fourth Actor:
 Oh, push me with one unconvulsive leap
 Against the point of this death-dealing blade!

Little Dog:
 Reeouw rrgh!

From *One Thousand Avant-Garde Plays* (Knopf, 1988).

Fourth Actor:
  Get that dog

Third Actor:
  Out of here

First and Second Actors:
  Get that noisome dog
  Out of the Theatre of Epidauros!

(*The god of medicine,* AESCULAPIUS, *comes onstage and picks up the* LITTLE DOG *in his arms.*)

Aesculapius:
  Come, my child, I shall shelter and guard you.
  No longer will anyone forget to take you out.
  And we will take long pleasant walks together—
  We'll leave this sickening theatre alone
  Where there is talk of nothing but family murder
  And devastation, relatives eating each other—
  It is enough to make even me, Aesculapius, sick at
      heart. . . . You, dog,
  Are the healthiest, most natural thing
  I have seen in this Epidauros Theatre in a long, long time.

(*The memory of his wife, who died young, momentarily comes back to* AESCULAPIUS.)
  Oh, Xanthia . . . *you*
  Were healthy, *you* were beautiful. When you died
  I stopped writing plays myself, and became a doctor. . . .
  Oh, well . . . things long ago! Come, pleasant dog,
  Now shall we make the paths of Greece our friends.

(AESCULAPIUS *and the* DOG *go off.* ACTORS *continue rehearsing lines.*)

Second Actor:
  This hand has choked the one who gave me life—I
      smelled her dying . . .

First Actor:
   He slaughtered his own child—and mine—our daughter,
   To calm the Thracian winds—

Third Actor (*as* ORESTES, *looking back behind him and seeing the* FURIES):
   You can't see them, but *I* see them. They are after me! I
      can't stay a moment more!

(*The* THIRD ACTOR *runs off screaming. The* FIFTH ACTOR *enters, attired as* OEDIPUS, *blinded, with blood streaming from his eye sockets.*)

Fifth Actor:
   Apollo did not do this.

The Taps

(CITIZENS *come tap-dancing down the street, behaving in uncontrolled, wild, and lawless ways.*)

Citizens:
  Tap tap, tap-tap-tap-tap
  Tap tap, tap-tap-tap-tap

Dionysios (*looking at them with great disapproval*):
  Oof! What a state the world is in—look at them!
  What we need is a Poet
  Whose works are full of good, old-fashioned wisdom,
  Someone to teach them how to live and act. The best are
    dead, though—
  We'll have to go to Hell to get one back.

Xanthios:
  How will we get there?

(*Enter, with a* CORPSE, *a tap-dancing* FUNERAL PROCESSION.)

Funeral Procession:
  Tap tap-tap-tap, tap-tap tap-tap
  Tap tap-tap-tap, tap-tap, tap-tap

Dionysios:
  We'll follow that corpse. I'm sure he's headed there.

From *One Thousand Avant-Garde Plays* (Knopf, 1988).

(*They tap-dance after the* PROCESSION. *The scene changes to Hades. It's very dark.*)

Dionysios (*to* DIS, *God of the Underworld*):
O God of this Great Place,
We need a Poet, and all the best are here.

Dis:
Take any one you like. They're not much good here—
always reciting.
(*calling*) Poets! Eliot! Stevens! Yeats!
There's someone here to see you.

(*The* POETS *appear.*)

Dionysios:
I want to take one of you back to earth.
But how to decide? Which one? Why don't you each
recite
One or two of your verses, and I'll choose.

(*Each* POET *in turn mounts a little podium and recites.*)

Yeats:
I have coom all this distance, lookin for faeryland.

Eliot:
I sometimes wonder if that is what Krishna meant
Among other things—or one way of putting the same
thing—

Stevens:
Chieftain Iffucan of Azcan in caftan
Of tan with henna hackles, halt!

Dionysios:
By God! I'll take all three!

Dis:
Good journey back!

(DIONYSIOS, XANTHIOS, YEATS, ELIOT, *and* STEVENS *climb up out of Hades toward the Earth. At last, a little light begins to show.*)

Dionysios:
    Come, Poets, into the day!

(*Faint, and then louder and louder sounds of tap-dancing, as* CITIZENS *approach to hear them.*)

Chatting with a Chinese Philosopher

"COMPARATIVELY—COMPARATIVELY," ANNOUNCED Ni-Shu, "the poetry of Keats and Shelley can scarcely be compared. However, since I am one of the few critics (I think!) who very clearly prefer the work of Shelley to that of mountain Keats, I must blue birds begin with rotten straphangers as the Yugoslavian boat 'sinks'; it dives into the ocean, and when it re-emerges, Nineveh is on deck, by copulation submerged."

Go on with your criticism, said Santa, it seems to me you are getting lost in that part.

Yes, said Chen-yu.

Ni-Shu said, It is all a part of that. It is a new kind of a criticism.

Santa: Well, so . . .

"Keats sees a flower. What does he do? He smells it, perhaps tastes it even, stares at it, sees its purples and its reds, and even hears its motion in the light, close-to-the-ground breeze. Thus in his poems we FEEL like a flower—or so it would seem. But the impression is false. A flower does not know how it smells and tastes, or even how it looks. Can you say you know the same about yourself? Shelley comes upon a flower and it is mere radiance, mere language; there is no intention whatsoever that we be made to feel exactly how the flower feels and smells: what it IS to be a flower. And thus by not trying this he accomplishes it, Shelley does. There is this radiance, this piece of word, this language fragment floating around, I am sure it is exactly how a flower feels. It's how I feel."

From *The Red Robins* (Random House, 1975).

94

I think he is right, said Jill. How nice to get a Chinese viewpoint on our own literature.

Are you English? asked Ni-Shu.

No, American, said Jill, as are a number of us here; but we consider that a part of "our" literature anyway.

"Actually it is very far from being so," said Ni-Shu; "there is probably a greater likeness between any two literatures of the world than there is between that of America and England. This is because the surface similarities are so great that the writer in either country (perhaps more particularly in the United States) is not driven to express himself *peculiarly* in what amounts to a totally radical fashion. That is to say, the writer does not need to find the exact words for every thing, kind of person, and action and then fit them all together to make a whole and coherent truth. Already given a language that had partly done this (for its past, at least, for it is a process which must be continually re-done) the American writer, in being able to dispense with the central, nay crucial nub of the creative process, has created a literature unrivaled anywhere for its weirdness and for the apparently helter-skelter triviality of its concerns. It is like the sort of bread that might be baked by a baker who had already been given the crusts. Very much like that. So not only the content but even the *surface* of American books is utterly mystifying! But these books, to return to my main point, do come to bear certain (perhaps accidental) resemblances to the literatures of such out-of-the-way places as Africa and the Far East, but they will never resemble any English work until they have fled full circle, perhaps all the way around the globe: through Irish, Finnish, Hindustani, Turkish, Melanesian, Afghan, Japanese, and so forth. For English is what the American 'language' or literature is being created FROM, therefore of necessity by very definition fleeing from. Much American snobbery consists in trying to be English, but the snob would be spending his time far better if he would begin being Finn or Afghan, for it is only through that path, in that direction, that he shall ever succeed in his goal of becoming English."

Do you think that our travels are making us more English? asked Jill.

I don't know, said the Chinese philosopher. Do you want to be?

I don't know, Jill said. But not all of us are American. Bud is German, and we're all of very varied descent.

Yes, all you Americans are, said Ni-Shu. Well, now I must be going. Come, Chen-yu. Santa Claus, it has been a great pleasure to hear the opinions of your young people.

It has been OUR great pleasure to listen to you, Master, said Santa Claus. And he very politely took them to the door, where the President was waiting for them in a big snowy plane with deep-blue upholstered seats.

Goodbye, Santa, said Ni-Shu, climbing into the cockpit beside the President; and "Goodbye" sang Chen-yu. "Don't forget us at Christmas time, Santy," laughed the President, and the plane sped away.

My God I'm bored, said Lyn.

Lyn! Jill looked at her a little sternly. Jill, that's not fair! I thought it was loads of fun and very interesting.

There is something in what she says, Bud said in a husky German accent.

It reminded me somewhat of the message we derived out of the Japanese Noh players, Bob said, staring out sleepily now at the misty white elephant tusks which symbolized that the dawn was once again to be difficult and bloody. But we had better be getting a little sleep. There is difficult work to be done for the raid of tomorrow. Full of thought, we turned in.

Four Modern Poets

Mending Sump

"Hiram, I think the sump is backing up.
The bathroom floor boards for above two weeks
Have seemed soaked through. A little bird, I think,
Has wandered in the pipes, and all's gone wrong."
"Something there is that doesn't hump a sump,"
He said; and through his head she saw a cloud
That seemed to twinkle. "Hiram, well," she said,
"Smith is come home! I saw his face just now
While looking through your head. He's come to die
Or else to laugh, for hay is dried-up grass
When you're alone." He rose, and sniffed the air.
"We'd better leave him in the sump," he said.

Robert Frost

From *On the Great Atlantic Rainway* (Knopf, 1994).

Canto CXXIII

Ava piece a banana BOYZ sed the Commish
                              PONG CHOOEY
Ternight yer in fer a real treat
                    and alla manyata
            stripped down to her knees and there a mantle
            a mantle of finest ivory that Casticcini made or Ezra
Let us alone / or like Yeatsy "Let me
ALONE" and Radinbranath in Terhune
reading the Chicago papers and asking after Minsky
the burlesk Minsky BANG GONG   and the gold dust
                                    hit in the face
his teeth broken his gold teeth broken O Anna Magnani
the pity that has broken my doily
            SAITH Themis   and
   my rock garden is empty no flower
            nor beast pusheth
                        because of phooey
            Phooey hath eaten my garden
                        Evil the cowslip
            and the gem
                  that are tainted with phooey
                        dit Wang Chu
                        972 B.C.
And you will grow up to be a high commercial
So that people of esteem will read your verses
Then you shall return to this valley and teach eating
                  For who hath eaten phooey
                  Returneth not unto paradise
Dem mudder fuckers doan unnerstan me
Said the Princess Toy Ling A.D. 1922
Dey doan unnerstan nuttin but smut

That was the year the doves fell at Livorgno
Six thousand of them and Caspia walking among them
From morning till night until finally there was nothing
But her feet and then nothing
But her ankles as white as doves
                            nothing but ankles moving
            I have brought these jewels to Mantua
            I have been fortunate in my choice of birds
    for this beak eateth phooey
                        PING CHONG
for this beak eateth Ping Chong phooey.
                                        Ezra Pound

From *Kulchur* 2, no. 5 (spring 1962).

Pat

Desperate, rough, good at boat-handling, Pat you devil,
  you Irish devil,
I remember the day you came to me with a baby mouse
  in your hand
And a question so fancifully, beautifully formed, to be
  civil
To me, to me your confessor, and said, "Father, the
  damned
Beast, will it walk, ever? for holding it I have been,
  complaining not, still
'Tis hot, in palm, and awkward for boat-handling,
  plover
's egg nor duck-roach more forceful to induce chill
Of fear to nary handle boat well; yet found, picked up
  amid clover

Does hang to me, Father, Father, to press it
Ever in protecting hands, or can that, that Nature that
  first formed it
Keep it, keep it in all its mousehood, sweet now, swift
  Jack mouse-ship; unless it
Can, shall, nary a drop shall I it ever, but always,
  Father, it keep." I, "Pat, what warmed it
First, not these fingers, these good pounce shingles,
  shatter-brads to ship—these, answer! were *they*
  mothers
Its, or, aye, some more rock-warmed, sea-formed His?
  Tell." You, ah, to knee dropped, dropped, flung it,
  flung flung hence, then "Praise! Not! not these!
  Others!"

Gerard Manley Hopkins

I Like Rats

I never saw a rat
Sorry for itself.
I never saw two rats
Consoling one another for being rats.

Rats live good full rat-lives with other rats.
Rat mind and rat heart plunge them into rat sex with
    other impassioned rats.
People say they are poison and ugly and cause disease.
I say people cause disease.
I never caught a cold or syphillis or gonorrhea or
    manic depression from a rat.

D. H. Lawrence

III

Teaching Great Poetry to Children

Giraffes, how did they make Carmen? Well, you see, Carmen
ate the prettiest rose in the world and then just then the
great change of heaven occurred and she became the pret-
tiest girl in the world and because I love her.

Lions, why does your mane flame like fire of the devil? Be-
cause I have the speed of the wind and the strength of the
earth at my command.

Oh Kiwi, why have you no wings? Because I have been born
with the despair to walk the earth without the power of
flight and am damned to do so.

Oh bird of flight, why have you been granted the power to
fly? Because I was meant to sit upon the branch and to be
with the wind.

Oh crocodile, why were you granted the power to slaughter
your fellow animal? I do not answer.

Chip Wareing, 5th grade, PS 61

From *Rose, Where Did You Get that Red?* (Random House, 1973).

1

Last year at PS 61 in New York City I taught my third-through-sixth-grade students poems by Blake, Donne, Shakespeare, Herrick, Whitman, William Carlos Williams, Wallace Stevens, John Ashbery, and Federico García Lorca. For several years before, I had been teaching poetry writing to many of these children, and they liked it so much that I thought there must be a way to help them read and enjoy great poetry by adults.

I found a way to do it, in conjunction with my students' own writing, which enabled the children to get close to the adult poems and to understand and enjoy them. What I did, in fact, was to make these adult poems a part of their own writing. I taught reading poetry and writing poetry as one subject. I brought them together by means of "poetry ideas," which were suggestions I would give to the children for writing poems of their own in some way like the poems they were studying. We would read the adult poem in class, discuss it, and then they would write. Afterward, they or I would read aloud the poems they had written.

When we read Blake's "The Tyger" I asked my students to write a poem in which they were asking questions of a mysterious and beautiful creature. When we read Shakespeare's "Come Unto These Yellow Sands," I asked them to write a poem which was an invitation to a strange place full of colors and sounds. When we read Stevens's "Thirteen Ways of Looking at a Blackbird," I asked them to write a poem in which they talked about the same thing in many different ways. The problem in teaching adult poetry to children is that for them it often seems difficult and remote; the poetry ideas, by making the adult poetry to some degree part of an activity of their own, brought it closer and made it more accessible to them. The excitement of writing carried over to their reading; and the excitement of the poem they read inspired them in their writing.

I had used poetry ideas in teaching my students to write poetry before, to help them find perceptions, ideas, feelings, and new ways of saying things, and to acquaint them with some of the subjects and techniques they could bring into their poetry; I had proposed poems about wishes, dreams, colors, differences between the present and the past, poems which included a number of Spanish words, poems in which everything was a lie. I would often suggest ways of organizing the poem as well: for the Wish Poem, starting every line with "I wish"; to help them think about the difference between the present and the past, I suggested alternating line-beginnings of "I used to" and "But now"; for the Comparison Poem I suggested they put one comparison in every line, for a Color Poem the name of a color in every line. These formal suggestions were most often for some kind of repetition, which is natural to children's speech and much easier for them to use in expressing their feelings than meter and rhyme.

With the help of these poetry ideas, along with as free and inspiring a classroom atmosphere as I could create (I said they could make some noise, read each other's lines, walk around the room a little, and spell words as best they could, not to worry about it), and with a good deal of praise and encouragement from me and from each other, my students in grades one through six came to love writing poetry, as much as they liked drawing and painting, sometimes even more—

> The way I feel about art is nothing compared to the way I
>   feel about poetry.
> Poetry has something that art doesn't have and that's
>   feelings. . . .
>   Rafael Camacho, 6[1]

My poetry ideas were good ideas as long as they helped the children make discoveries and express feelings, which is what made them happy about writing—

> I like poetry because it puts me in places I like to be . . .
>   Tommy Kennedy, 6

---

1. The number following the child's name indicates the grade he or she was in when the poem was written.

You can express feelings non-feelings trees anything from A
    to Z that's why
IT'S GREAT STUFF!

Tracy Lahab, 6

They wrote remarkably well. Sometimes my students wrote poems without my giving them an idea, but usually they wanted one to help them get started to find new things to say.

Teaching students who were enthusiastic about poetry, good at writing it, and eager to get ideas for writing new poems, I considered the kind of poetry that they were usually taught in school (and the way it was taught) and I felt that an opportunity was being missed. Why not introduce them to the great poetry of the present and the past? It was a logical next step in the development of their own writing: it could give them new ideas for their poems, and it would be good in other ways too. If they felt a close relationship to adult poetry now, they could go on enjoying it and learning from it for a long time.

This result seemed unlikely to be produced by the poetry children were being taught in school. The poems my students wrote were better than most of those in elementary-school textbooks. Their poems were serious, deep, honest, lyrical, and formally inventive. Those in the textbooks seemed comparatively empty and safe. They characteristically dealt with one small topic in an isolated way—clouds, teddybears, frogs, or a time of year—

> . . . Asters, deep purple,
> A grasshopper's call,
> Today it is summer,
> Tomorrow is fall.[2]

Nothing was connected to any serious emotion or to any complex way of looking at things. Everything was reassuring and simplified, and also rather limited and dull. And there

---

2. From "September," *The World of Language,* Book 5. Follett Educational Corp.

was frequently a lot of rhyme, as much as possible, as though the children had to be entertained by its chiming at every moment. When Ron Padgett at PS 61 asked our fifth-grade students to write poems about spring, they wrote lines like these—

> Spring is sailing a boat
> Spring is a flower waking up in the morning
> Spring is like a plate falling out of a closet for joy
> Spring is like a spatter of grease . . .
> Jeff Morley, 5

Jeff deserved "When daisies pied and violets blue" and "When-as the rye reach to the chin" or William Carlos Williams's "Daisy" or Robert Herrick's "To Cherry Blossoms," rather than "September." If it was autumn that was wanted, I'm sure that with a little help, he could have learned something from "Ode to the West Wind" too. There is a condescension toward children's minds and abilities in regard to poetry in almost every elementary text I've seen:

> Words are fun! . . . Some giggle like tickles, or pucker like pickles, or jingle like nickels, or tingle like prickles. And then . . . your poem is done!
>   And so is my letter. But not before I wish you good luck looking through your magic window . . .[3]

says one author to third graders; but my third graders could write like this:

> I used to have a hat of hearts but now I have a hat of tears
> I used to have a dress of buttons but now I have a name of
>   bees . . .
> Ilona Baburka, 3

I had discovered that my students were capable of enjoying and also learning from good poetry while I was teaching them

---

3. "A Famous Author Speaks," *Our Language Today,* American Book Company.

writing. In one sixth-grade class I had suggested to the students a poem on the difference between the way they seemed to be to others and the way they really felt deep inside themselves. Before they wrote, I read aloud three short poems by D. H. Lawrence on the theme of secrecy and silence—"Trees in the Garden," "Nothing to Save," and "The White Horse." They liked the last one so much they asked me to read it three times:

> The youth walks up to the white horse, to put its halter on
> and the horse looks at him in silence.
> They are so silent they are in another world.

The Lawrence poems seemed to help the whole class take the subject of their poem seriously, and one girl, Amy Levy, wrote a beautiful and original poem which owed a lot to the specific influence of "The White Horse." She took from Lawrence the conception of another world coexistent with this one, which one can enter by means of secrecy and silence, and used it to write about her distance from her parents and the beauty and mystery of her own imaginings—

> We go to the beach
> I look at the sea
> My mother thinks I stare
> My father thinks I want to go in the water.
> But I have my own little world . . .[4]

In my new teaching my aim was to surround Amy, Ilona, Jeff, and the rest of my students with other fine poems, like Lawrence's, that were worthy of their attention and that could give them good experiences and help them in their own writing. Some of the poems would be much more difficult than "The White Horse," and all of them would probably be "too hard" for the children in some way, so I would not merely read the adult poems aloud but do all I could to make them clear and to bring the children close to them.

---

4. Amy's whole poem is in *Wishes, Lies, and Dreams,* p. 251.

I began with the general notion of teaching my students the poems I liked best, but I soon saw that some of these were better to teach than others. Some poems came to me right away because of some element in them that I knew children would be excited by and connect with their own feelings. The fantasy situation in Blake, for example, of talking to an animal—or the more real-life situation in Williams's "This Is Just to Say" of apologizing for something you're really glad you've done. Certain tones, too—Whitman's tone of boastful secret-telling. And strange, unexpected things, like Donne's comparisons of tender feelings to compasses and astronomical shifts.

Sometimes a particular detail of a poem made it seem attractive: the names of all the rivers in John Ashbery's "Into the Dusk-Charged Air"; the colors in Lorca's "Arbole, Arbole" and "Romance Sonambulo"; the animal and thing noises in Shakespeare's songs (bow-wow, ding-dong, and cock-a-doodle-dow).

Some poems had forms that suggested children's verbal games and ways children like to talk, such as the lists in Herrick's "Argument" and in Stevens's "Thirteen Ways of Looking at a Blackbird," or the series of questions in "The Tyger." Such forms would be a beginning for a poetry idea, since they were something the children could imitate easily when they wrote.

It was usually one of these appealing features that brought a poem into my mind as good to teach children. Of course, I wanted it to be a poem they could get a lot from. There are terrible poems about talking to animals and there are great ones. And the same for lists, strange comparisons, and the rest. I was looking for appealing themes and forms in the very best poems. "The Tyger," speaking to children's sense of strangeness and wonder, could heighten their awareness of nature and of their place in it. Herrick's "Argument" would help them to think about their poems in a new way, somewhat as they might think of places they had been or of specific things they had seen and done. Donne's poem could show them connections between supposedly disparate parts of their lives. Whitman could encourage them to trust their secret feelings about the world and how they were connected to it—it told them these feelings were more important than what they found in books. "Thirteen Ways of Looking at a Blackbird" showed the interest, the pleasure, and the intelligence of looking at the same thing in all kinds of ways. The Williams poems showed how poetry could be about very ordinary things. Ashbery's poem, like Donne's, could help them bring together a school subject—in this case, geography—in a playful and sensuous way with their feelings, and with poetry. One thing they could learn from them all was the importance of feelings and of one's secret imaginative life, which are so much what these poems are about. They were learning what great poetry had to do with them. Feelings they may have thought were silly or too private to be understood by anyone else were subjects that "great authors" wrote about. One reason I chose to teach Shakespeare was to show the children their connection to the poet they would be hearing about so often as the greatest who ever lived.

In deciding on poems, I wasn't put off by some of the difficulties teachers are often bothered by. Unfamiliar words and difficult syntax, for example, and allusions to unfamiliar things. My students learned new words and new conceptions in order to play a new game, or to enable them to understand science fiction in comics or on TV, so why not for poetry, which they liked just as much? Furthermore, since they were going to write poems themselves, the lesson did have something of the atmosphere of a game; and if they didn't find the poems as interesting as science fiction, I would have to figure out what was wrong with my teaching. In fact, in the excitement of reading the poems, the children were glad to learn the meanings of strange words, of old forms like *thee* and *thine,* and of strange conceptions like symmetry and sublunary.

I wasn't put off, either, by passages in a poem that I knew would remain obscure to them. To reject every poem the children would not understand in all its detail would mean eliminating too many good things. I knew they would enjoy and get something fine from Stevens's blackbird, even if the ironic allusiveness of "bawds of euphony" was going to escape them;

and I was sure they would be inspired by Donne's compass even though certain details about neo-Platonism and Ptolemaic astronomy would be too hard to explain.

Though it occurred to me, at first, to reject all poems with sex or religion as part of their subject, I decided it was all right to teach poems that dealt with these subjects in certain ways. The sexual theme in Donne's "Valediction" is implicit but not the main theme of the poem; the real emphasis is on love, the pain of parting, and the hope for reunion, all of which children can respond to. Blake's "The Tyger" is not sectarian in a way that might bother children, but touches on religious feelings of a more basic kind. Children can feel wonder and amazement and fear, and they are fascinated by superpowered beings; they can respond without difficulty to the Creator of the tyger.

Like its textural and thematic difficulties, a poem's length can make it seem impossible to teach to children. I thought if something about the poem was just right for my students, however, that it was all right to teach them only a part of it, which is what I did with "Song of Myself." I chose sections 1 and 2; in class I explained the relation of this part to the rest of the poem. There was no short poem of Whitman that I thought would teach them as much. I felt free also to select poems in another language if they had something fine in them for my students, as I thought several poems of Lorca did. I gave the children the poems in Spanish and in English translations. Translations are imperfect, and only a few children understood all the Spanish, but the good things here (the dreaminess, the music, the use of color, the contrast of original and translation itself) seemed to outweigh these disadvantages.

Rhymed poems and poems written in the language of the past could have had bad effects on my students' writing, but I didn't want to omit such poems. I dealt with rhyme by showing my students the other kinds of form there were in the rhymed poem—the series of questions, for example, in "The Tyger," and the repetition of words—and suggested they use that kind of form in the poems they wrote in the lesson. Along with the rhymed poems, I included some that didn't rhyme—those by Whitman, Stevens, Williams, and Ashbery. I explained the present-day equivalents of all out-of-date words and phrases in the poems, and, while the children wrote, I urged them to use the words they really used when they spoke. After five lessons on past poets, I did notice some conventional "literariness" in their language and in the subjects they wrote about. I didn't wish to discourage all literary imitation, since sometimes it helped the children to express genuine moods and feelings, such as awe and grandeur, which they might not have been able to express without it. However, I didn't want them to get lost in literariness. So I taught them Williams, who wrote in contemporary language about ordinary things. The example of a great poet who did this, I thought, would help the children do it for themselves.

What I saw in my students' own poetry was helpful to me in choosing poems to teach them. The extravagance of their comparisons in earlier poems ("The cat is as striped as an airplane take-off . . .") had something to do with my deciding on Donne. José Lopez's poem about talking to a dog ("Oh dog, how do you feel with so much hair around you?")[5] was one thing that put Blake's "The Tyger" in my mind. The tone of secrecy in the poems my students wrote inspired by Shakespeare's Songs made me think of teaching Whitman and of emphasizing a tone like that in his work. In writing for the Blake lesson, some children went backwards in the history of English poetry to an earlier style of talking to nature, lamenting mortality and whimsically inquiring into origins. "Rose, where did you get that red?" and, "Oh Daffodil I hope you never die but live forever!" showed me a connection I had never thought of and showed me, too, that my students might find it interesting to read Herrick.

The usual criteria for choosing poems to teach children are mistaken, if one wants poetry to be more than a singsong sort of Muzak in the background of their elementary education. It can be so much more. These criteria are total understandability, which stunts children's poetic education by giving them nothing to understand they have not already understood; "childlikeness" of theme and treatment, which condescends to

---

5. The "Cat" and Dog comparison are both in *Wishes, Lies, and Dreams.* p. 96 and p. 257.

their feelings and to their intelligence; and "familiarity," which obliges them to go on reading the same inappropriate poems their parents and grandparents had to read, such as "Thanatopsis" and "The Vision of Sir Launfal." One aspect of "childlikeness" that is particularly likely to work against children's loving poetry and taking it seriously is a cloyingly sweet and trouble-free view of life. Even Blake's "The Lamb," alone or in context with other sweet poems, could be taken that way. It is constant sweetness that is probably the main thing that makes boys, by the time they are in fifth or sixth grade, dislike poetry as something sissified and silly.

I ended up teaching, in this first series of lessons, three twentieth-century poets who wrote in English and one who wrote in Spanish; two poets who I suppose could be called Romantic—Blake and Whitman—one English, one American; two seventeenth-century poets; and Shakespeare. There was nothing of a survey about what I did. My point was to introduce my students to a variety of poetic experiences. Other teachers will doubtless want to try other poems. There are many poems children can learn from, and a teacher has a pleasantly wide choice.

3

When I became interested in teaching a particular poem, I would look for a poetry idea to go with it, such as, for the Blake class, "Imagine you are talking to a mysterious and beautiful creature and you can speak its secret language, and you can ask it anything you want." The poetry idea, as I've said, was to give the students a way to experience, while writing, some of the main ideas and feelings in the poem we were studying.

Usually one of the same features that attracted me to a poem as a good one to teach would furnish me with the start of the poetry idea. The poetry idea for Herrick's "Argument" would obviously include "Make a list of things you've written poems about"; that for Stevens would begin, "Talk about the same thing in a number of different ways." The poetry idea for Whitman would have something to do with secrets. That for Shakespeare, with noises; for Lorca, with colors; for Ash-

9/

Venice. July 3rd 1818

1.

Southey! you are a poet — poet Laureat —
And representative of all the race —
Although 'tis true you turned out a Tory at
Last — it has lately been my common case
But more ~~~~~~ ~~~~~~ my epic thorougode! — what are you at.
With you all the Romans in & out of place?
A nest of tuneful persons, to my eye
"Like four and twenty Blackbirds in a pye —"

"Which pye being opened they began to sing" —
~~In the old song~~ (This old song to new ~~~~~~ holds good)
"A dainty dish to set before the King"
{ Or Regent who admires such kind of food } —
~~And~~ Coleridge too has lately taken wing,
But like a Hawk encumbered with his hood,
Explaining Metaphysics to the Nation —
I wish he would explain his explanation. —

3.

And Wordsworth in a rather long "Excursion"
{I think the Quarto holds five hundred pages}
Has given a ~~~~~~ sample, from the vasty
of his new System ~~~~~~ the Pages
to perplex

George Gordon, Lord Byron FROM Don Juan

Ricky

Little flower good flower

Mice Mice Mice Why do you
look nice? squeak squeak! Mice Mi
Mice Mice squeak squeak squeak.
Why your eyes are red? squeak? do you
sleep in a bed? Where did you get ruby
eyes? squeak squeak squeak squeak
squeak squeak mouse mouse mousee
eeeeeeeeeeeeeeeeeeeeeeeeeeeeeeeeeeeeee

SQUEAK
MOUSE

Ricky Marcilla, 3rd Grade,
poem inspired by William Blake's *The Tyger*.

The Hand-writing of John Keats.
(witness) Charles Cowden Clarke.

Give me a golden pen and let me lean
~~On heaped up flowers in regions clear and calm~~
~~Bring me a tablet whiter than~~ palm
Of a young angel what time it is seen

Give me a golden pen and let me lean   far
On heaped up flowers in regions clear and clear
Bring me a Tablet whiter than a Star
Or palm of ~~young self~~ hymning angel when it is seen
The ~~silver~~ things of heavenly harp atween
And let their glide by many a pearly car
Pink ~~robes~~ and flowing hair and ~~softest~~ diamond
And half-~~seen~~ through glossy wings, and glances keen
The while let Music wander round my ears
And as it reaches each delicious ~~close~~ ending
Let me write down a line of glorious tone
And full of many wonders of the spheres—
~~Tingling~~
For what a height my Spirit is contending
'Tis not content so soon to be alone—

John Keats *Sonnet XII*

fear.   Vilma

I
feared
my
Shadow
But
It
was
nice
to
see
my
self
in
fear.

Vilma Mejias, 6th Grade, *Fear*
inspired by William Carlos William's
The Locust Tree in Flower.

Ah, not ~~that~~ granite dead and (cold) cold!

Ah, not ~~that~~ granite dead and cold!
Far far from ~~its~~ base and shaft expanding — the
~~limited~~ round zones circling, comprehending
~~No~~ lurid fame exceptional, ~~poor~~ ~~monstrous~~ in

tellest nor conquest domination ~~in entire~~
Thou Washington art all the worlds ~~a~~ — not
yours alone. ~~but~~ America
in every
Europe's as well in ~~castle~~ or in laborers cot —
Or ~~from~~ the Arabs in his tent — the African's
Old Asia's there with venerable smile seated
amid her ruins.

Great the antique ~~the~~ hero new? 'tis but the
same — the indomitable heart and arm — the
heir legitimate — ~~the same~~ ~~unbroken~~ line
Courage, alertness, patience, hope, the same — cen
in defeat defeated not the same;)

Wherever ship, ~~sails~~, or house is built on land,
or night or day,
Through teeming cities' streets, indoors or out,
factories or farms,
Now, or to come, or past — wherever patriot
wills existed or exist
Wherever Freedom, poised by Toleration, swayed
by Law. ~~in them~~ from them,
~~Rising or risen~~ there's thy ~~true~~ ~~monument~~
Rises or is rising thy true monument,
stands or

Walt Whitman FROM *Ode to Washington*

① Gravity

love is like gravity pulling adeversed
apple together. because when we're
seperate we are pulled together
aging

② mornin dew

love is like a soft mornin dew
which has a magic formula which makes
Love appere

③ fourgive and fourget

④ Love = 2 planets joining to make
a eclips
Love = a rocketship going to the
moon when the astrohants sees
venus the capsule goes crazy now
hits venas es shade and what
augly venas the the ship takes off

Miklos Lengyel, 6th Grade,
poem inspired by John Donne's
A Validiction: Forbidding Mourning.

bery, with the names of rivers. The poetry idea would also have to connect the poem to the children's feelings and include suggestions for a form in which they would enjoy writing. So I would work out and elaborate my first conception for a poetry idea until I could give it to the children in a way that would immediately make it interesting and make them eager to write.

Some poems presented no problem. Once the children saw what they were about, they were eager to write poems like them of their own. This was the case with "This Is Just to Say." Apologizing for something they were secretly glad they had done was so familiar and amusing an experience that in order to inspire them to write about it I had only to show them what the poem was about. Ashbery's river poem had an equally obvious and immediate appeal just as it was, a poem with a different river in every line. In this case, however, I was a little afraid of a merely mechanical response, so I said "Write a poem with a river in every line, and really imagine you are seeing the river or are floating on it, and say how it really looks and feels. If you want to, put in colors and sounds and times of year. Think what color each river is, what kind of sound it makes, what month of the year it reminds you of." Ashbery's poem doesn't include such details about each river, but thinking about such details helped the children go from one real, sensuous experience of a river to another—"Delaware—green with April birds and flowers / Missouri—red January bugs and laughter. . . ." (*Mayra Morales, 5*).

Herrick's poem, like Ashbery's, had something immediately appealing for the children to imitate: a list of subjects they had written poems about. However, to enjoy making such a list, as Herrick evidently did, a child would have to be in a similarly pleasantly expansive and satisfied state of mind. I could help to make children feel this way by reminding them of the poems they had written for me about colors, noises, wishes, lies, and dreams. I could suggest they think, too, of their poems in more detail. Had they written, as Herrick says he has, of flowers? of girls? of love? of things to eat and drink? That was good as far as it went, but some of the children had written only a very few poems. To help them out, and to give to everyone's poem more of the impetus of pleasure and desire, I made it part of the poetry idea that, along with writing of what they had already written about, they could say what they would like to write about in the future. This makes the poem more exciting.

Williams's "Between Walls" had an appealing idea—something supposed to be ugly which really is beautiful—but the children would get more out of it if I could connect it to their feelings as well. I did that by using the words *really* and *secretly*, which I found as helpful here as, in other lessons, appealing to the children's senses and asking them to think of colors and sounds. My suggestion was, "Write a poem about something that is supposed to be ugly, but which you *really secretly* think is beautiful, as Williams thinks the broken glass shining in back of the hospital is beautiful." Another time *secret* was a help was in the Blake class, when, to make the children believe more in the reality of the situation (their talking to an animal or other creature), I said that they should pretend they could speak its secret language.

I saw right away that Shakespeare's "Come Unto These Yellow Sands" was attractive to children for its gaiety and for its use of sounds, but I didn't find a way to connect it to their feelings until I began to think about its being an invitation and how exciting the situations of inviting and being invited are for children. Invitations are connected with birthdays and all sorts of mysteries and surprises. My poetry idea, which helped the children get the genuine strangeness of this and other Shakespearean songs, was to write a poem inviting people to a strange and beautiful place, full of wonderful sounds.

Sometimes my students' reactions would lead me to change the poetry idea. In the Blake class my poetry idea was to ask a creature questions. Several children asked me if they could put in the answers, too. I said yes. Though including answers would make a poem less like Blake's on the surface, it could make it more like his in a more important way if it helped the child believe in the human/animal conversation. Conversations are easier to believe in if someone answers. Another question in the Blake class was "Can we talk to a different creature in every line?" I agreed to this, too. It would make the poem easier for those children who that day didn't feel up to sustaining a whole poem about one animal, bird, or insect and might help them refresh their inspiration in every line. And Blake himself had addressed a number of different creatures in *Songs of Innocence and Experience*.

These variations of the poetry ideas weren't false to the poems except in insignificant ways. I didn't want a poetry idea which commanded a child to closely imitate an adult poem. That would be pointless. I wanted my students to find and to re-create in themselves the main feelings of the adult poems. For this purpose, a lot of freedom in the poetry idea was necessary. They would need to be free, too, from demands of rhyme and meter, which at their age are restrictions on the imagination; and from the kinds of tone and subject matter which might oppress them. In relation to "The Tyger," this meant suggesting they write a poem in the form of repeated questions rather than asking for five stanzas of couplet-rhymed tetrameter; and that they write about talking to a strange creature, rather than that they write about The Wonders of God's Creation.

I could be fairly sure I had a good poetry idea worked out when examples of lines to illustrate it came easily to me. If I could think of lines inviting people to strange places or of ugly things that are really beautiful or of comparisons between geometry and magnetism and how I felt about someone, the children, with my help, would be able to as well. The final test of the idea, though, would be in class—if my suggestions for a poem weren't exciting and clear to the children, then I would have to find a way to make them so.

There are, of course, different writing suggestions, different poetry ideas that one can use with a particular poem. I approached the wonder and amazement in Blake through the theme of talking to an animal. My own childhood had been colored by the fantastic hope that I would be able to speak to animals and birds and share my feelings with them and find out their secrets, and this was one thing that made me feel my students might respond well to this particular idea. But I could just as well have approached the wonder and amazement through the theme of origins, of thinking of all the strange things in the world and imagining how they were made. Or by the theme of marveling at the superpowered being who does everything that is done in the world. In such a poem, for example, each line might begin with, "Who would dare . . . ?" and the children could be helped to begin by a few examples like "Who would dare to make a tiger?": Who would dare to lift the red-hot sun out of the street every morning? Who would dare to push the electricity through the subway tracks? Who would dare to go out into the middle of the ocean and push the waves to shore?

Writing suggestions have been used with teaching poetry before. Those I have seen in textbooks, however, are unhelpful either because they don't give the child enough (Write a Poem of Your Own about a Tiger), or bad because they give him too much—often, for example, telling him what to feel—(Write a Poem about How Beautiful You Think Some Animal Is). "Write a Poem in Which You Imagine Talking to an Animal" is in the right direction, but not dramatic enough. A writing suggestion should help a child to feel excited and to think of things he wants to write.

4

I would go to my classes at PS 61 with copies of poems for everyone. I would pass them out and ask the children to read them. I would tell the children that I would explain what was unclear to them in the poetry and that after we had discussed it they would write poems of their own that were like it in some way. Interested, as they always were, in anything connected with their writing, my students read the work to themselves, then listened to me read it aloud, and our discussion began.

When I talked about the poems, I tried to make the children feel close to them in every way I could. The fact that they were going to write a poem connected to the one we studied was a start. Beyond that, I wanted to make the poem as understandable as possible, and also as real, tangible, and dramatic as I could. I wanted to create excitement about it there in the classroom. When I could judge from what the children said and from their mood in general that they had understood the poem and its connection to themselves and to things they wanted to say themselves, I would have them write.

Many details of adult poetry are difficult for children, but they are glad to have them explained if they are interested in the poem, and if they aren't made to feel that the poem is over their heads. I immediately made the dramatic situation of the poem clear, often by a few questions. Who is Blake talking to? Why does he think that the tiger is "burning"? I responded in a positive way to all their answers; even wrong answers would show them thinking about the poem and using their ingenuity, trying to understand. Once started on that path, with my help and that of their classmates, they eventually understood. As soon as I could, I would begin to associate the poem with their own experience. Have you ever talked with a cat or a dog? Have you ever seen its eyes in the dark? Did they shine like those of the tiger? Unfamiliar words, such as *fearful* and *frame,* and odd syntactical constructions, such as "What dread hand? and what dread feet?" I treated as small impediments in the way of enjoying the big experience of the poem, to be dealt with as quickly as possible. I explained them briefly and went on.

Along with doing all I could to make the poem available and easy, I did things in every class to dramatize the poem and make the children excited about it. When we came to Blake's lines about the creation of the tiger's heart, "And what shoulder, and what art / Could twist the sinews of thy heart?" I asked the children to close their eyes, be quiet, put their fingers in their ears, and listen hard: that strange, muffled thumping they heard was their heart—how must Blake have felt imagining the tiger's heart, which was probably even stranger? To dramatize Donne's compass image and show the children how it really worked, I brought a big compass to school and showed them what his comparison was about in every detail. In the Lorca class, to help them feel the music and the magical use of colors, I had the children close their eyes and listen while I said words in English and in Spanish, such as "green" and *"verde,"* and asked questions such as

"Which word is greener? Which is brighter?" To excite the children about Williams's "The Locust Tree in Flower," I began by having the whole class write a poem like it together, the children shouting out lines to me, which I wrote on the blackboard. In the Ashbery class I had the children call out to me the names of all the rivers they could think of. In the Herrick class, they named the things they had written about and the things they wanted to write about.

The discussion of some poems went more quickly than that of others. The discussion of the Williams poems, for example, was very brief. After a few readings and a few questions, the children seemed really to have a sense of the poems and to be ready to write. They were starting their own poems five minutes after the class began. I spent a good deal more time discussing "The Tyger." I wanted to be sure to communicate to the children the main feelings in the poem—fear, amazement, and wonder—which seemed less accessible to them than the main feelings in "Between Walls" and "This Is Just to Say." It seemed good to linger over particular parts of the poem to make them dramatic and real—the tiger's burning, the forests of the night, the fire in the tiger's eyes, the making of the tiger's brain in a furnace. Even my explanation of *symmetry*, a word none of my students knew, helped to involve them in the poem. I showed them that they themselves were symmetrical, and—excitedly touching their own shoulders, elbows, ears, and knees—they could feel the strangeness of the tiger's symmetry, too. I didn't think it necessary to teach every detail of a poem, just those that would help give the children a true sense of its main feelings.

Once they had that sense, I would give them the poetry idea; sometimes I would have given them a suggestion of it earlier in the lesson, so they could think about it while going over the poem. Now I had to make sure that it was clear enough to help them write a poem. First I would explain the idea, then answer questions about it; then give the children a few examples of how it would work out, what kinds of subjects they might deal with, what kinds of lines they might write. When I had suggested a few possibilities, like, "You can compare you and your girlfriend or boyfriend to magnets," or

"You can ask questions like 'Lion, where did your terrible roar come from?' " I would ask the children for ideas and sample lines of their own. When these came to them easily, and when a lot of hands were raised in the air to give me more and more of them, that is, when the children were obviously understanding the project and full of ideas, I would pass out paper and they would write.

This writing part of the lesson was the same as it had been in my classes on teaching poetry writing alone, without adult poetry. The children talked, laughed, looked at each other's poems, called me to their desk to read and to admire, or, if they were "stuck," to give them ideas. It was a happy, competitive, creative atmosphere, and I was there to praise them, encourage them, and inspire them. When a student finished a poem quickly, I would sometimes suggest he write another. Some sixth graders were so excited about Williams's "This Is Just to Say" that they rapidly wrote three or four poems, apologizing to their dog, their fish, their parents, and their friends—to the dog, perhaps, for eating its biscuit, to the fish for forgetting to feed it, to their mother for breaking a dish, to a friend for eating the flowers off his head. In the Lorca class, if they had finished quickly, I asked those children who had written their poems all in Spanish to take another sheet of paper and write a translation. Sometimes when a child felt seriously impeded, I'd suggest he write a poem in collaboration with somebody else, or I would write one with him myself, which is how Rosa Rosario and I wrote "Poem: At six o'clock. . . ." My aim in general was to move around enough and respond enough to what the children were writing to keep things going happily all over the room.

I wanted to keep the free and pleasant atmosphere my students had always had in which to write poetry. There was no reason why the presence of great poems should interfere with that. I did everything I could in our discussion to make the poem seem easy and familiar to them. Now, while they wrote, I let the poetry idea take over from the adult poem, and their own ideas lead them in various directions. In the Blake class: Yes, you can talk to a stone if you wish, instead of an animal. Yes, Markus, you can write it in "octopus language." Yes, you can, instead of asking the animal questions, tell it what to do. I would stress, all the while, the part of it I thought would most inspire them: But remember, whatever you do, that you are really talking to it—really. I said yes, too, to my Spanish-speaking students, in the Lorca class, who wanted to write their whole poems in Spanish instead of just using Spanish words for colors. And to Yuk, a Chinese girl in the same fifth-grade class, who asked if, instead of Spanish words, she could use Chinese color words in her poem. When I praised the children's lines, it was not for their resemblance to Blake or to Donne, but for what they were in themselves— sometimes very much like the work of the poet we started with and sometimes less so—

> Giraffe! Giraffe!
> What kicky, sticky legs you've got.
> What a long neck you've got. It looks like a stick of fire. . . .
>
> Hipolito Rivera, 6

The adult poem started them off, but this part was all their own, and had to be, otherwise the lesson would come to nothing. Forced imitation could make them hate the adult poem rather than like it and wouldn't bring them close to it. But the energy and volatility of their imagination were a different kind of educational force. Anything the poem started in their imagination, and wherever it took them, I thought was fine.

To help them be free as they wrote, I urged them to write mainly in their own language, rather than in that of the poem, if it was from an earlier time. Rhyme, as I have said, I told them they needn't use. And, as in all my poetry classes, I asked them not to worry about spelling (or punctuation or neatness). All that could be corrected later. De-emphasizing these mechanical aspects of writing makes it easier for everyone to write and makes it possible thereby for some children who would not otherwise have dared to write poetry to write it and to come to love it; I had children like this, in fact, terrible spellers, who developed into fine and enthusiastic poets, and into students with more confidence in themselves as well.

The children usually wrote for about fifteen minutes. I

tried to give everybody time to finish, though if one or two children were still writing after everyone else was waiting to give me his poem, I collected all but theirs and let them go on writing. Sometimes I would read the poems aloud to the class. More often the children would read them themselves—they had come to enjoy doing that quite a lot. Afterward I would mimeograph their poems and include among them the adult work we had studied. Blake's "The Tyger" would be there between Loraine Fedison's "Oh Ants Oh Ants" and Hipolito Rivera's "Giraffe! Giraffe!" and, I felt pretty sure, somewhere in everyone's memory and imagination as a real and vivid experience.

To help children write well and enjoy it, perhaps the most important thing to do, I found, is to be positive about everything. I responded appreciatively to what they said and to what they wrote. Everything had some value, the very fact they could imagine talking to an animal, anything at all they found to say to it. So encouraged, they could go on to do more. Poetry writing is a talent that thrives, in children at any rate, on responsiveness and praise. If I preferred some lines or ideas to others, I responded more enthusiastically to those, rather than criticizing the ones I liked less.

I was assured the children were learning something by their continuing interest in class and by the poems they wrote. Sometimes a child wrote a poem that showed a remarkable mastery of a particular poet's way of seeing and experiencing things—

Goldglass

In the back yard
Lies in the sun
White glass
Reflecting the sun

Marion Mackles, 6

Marion's poem, written in a class on William Carlos Williams, shows not only William's attention to the beauty of small and supposedly unbeautiful things, but also his way of making the poem, as it goes along, a physical experience of discovery for the reader. Sometimes what the children wrote would be in many ways unlike the adult poetry we read, yet obviously inspired by it, as were a number of poems written in the Shakespeare class, poems about escaping into freedom: freedom from school; freedom from the powerlessness of childhood; freedom, even, from ordinary reality—

Oh come with me to see a Daisy. . . .
And put a lion on the chair and let teacher sit on it . . .
. . . and let her give no homework for the rest of the year . . .

Andrea Dockery, 5

We'll fly away, over mountains and hills.
And then for us the world will stand still.
The world will be at our command . . .

Maria Gutierrez, 5

We are free, free, come, come, I am inviting you to the land
of freedom where dogs go quack quack instead of bow,
wow, bark, bark. . . .

Rosa Rosario, 5

Of course, I didn't give quizzes or tests of any kind on poetry. A few bad marks would have made poetry, for most of my students, an enemy. But though few had the critical skill to say much about the poems we read, they all could experience them. For the space of reading the Blake poems and writing Blake-like poems of their own, the children were confronting tigers; they were talking to nature; they were lifted out of their ordinary selves by the magic of what they were saying; the fresh power of their feelings and perceptions was, for a moment, a real power in the world. One may feel, as a poet I know said to me, that "some things should be saved for later." Some things inevitably will be, because there are aspects of Blake's "The Tyger" and Donne's "Valediction" that elementary-school children won't respond to. But to save the whole poems for later means that some important things will be lost, permanently—the experience, for example, of responding to Blake's poem when one is ten years old and can still half believe that one's girlfriend was created by a magical transformation and that one can talk to a lion about its speed and its strength; or the experience of "Come Unto These Yellow Sands," when one can believe in the magic of dancing oneself into oneness with nature; or reading John Donne when rocketry and desire can be thought of together in an unaffected way.

All these are good experiences to have. When a child has had a few of them, he may begin to anticipate finding more of them in poetry and want to read more of it, rather than being cut off from it, as so many schoolchildren now are. My students, of course, were also being helped as writers. The adult poems added good things to their own work. When they picked up their pencils to write now, there were a few more tones they could take, more ways to organize a poem, new kinds of subject matter they could bring in.

<h1 style="text-align:center">6</h1>

Different children did their best work at different times. A few young poets suddenly came to life in the class on William Carlos Williams's "This Is Just to Say"; I suspect it was the naughtiness theme (apologizing but really glad) that did it. Some Spanish-speaking students wrote their best work in the Lorca class, obviously delighted at the chance to read a poem in school in their language and to be able to use Spanish in their own poems. Some classes were altogether better than others. The children's responses to Blake and Donne were especially strong and convincing, whereas I felt my students had not gotten as much as they might have from Stevens. I thought of a better way to teach Stevens only afterward.[6] Sometimes even with the best of poems and poetry ideas, a poetry class would go badly; the children would be tired or out of sorts, or I would be, and the enthusiasm and excitement conducive to writing poems wouldn't be there. Some-

---

6. Usually when I had ideas for improving a lesson, I'd have a chance to try it again. Often, when I taught two or three different classes (of different children) in succession, the later ones would profit from what I'd learned in the earlier.

times a lesson picked up suddenly after a good idea that some student or I had; at other times it seemed best to put off poetry till the next day. In any case, a dull class doesn't mean that children "aren't really interested" in poetry, but only that something is interfering with their feeling that interest as strongly as they might.

The differences between grades were like those I had already noticed in teaching writing. Third- and fourth-graders tended to be more exuberant, bouncy, and buoyant than their more serious older schoolmates. One of their characteristic reactions was to write "joke poems," which made fun of some aspect of the poem or of my poetry idea—of talking to an animal in its secret language, for example, in the lesson on Blake—"Glub blub, little squid. Glub blub, why blub do you glub have blub glubblub blub such glub inky stuff blubbb? . . ." (Markus Niebanck) or in the same lesson, of the strangeness of creatures—"Little duck, little duck, how did you get those iron legs? / How did you get those steel eyes? . . ." (Edgar Guadeloupe). These were fine responses to the poems and I showed my appreciation of them. Wildness and craziness and silliness were means for all my students to make contact with their own imaginations and through them with the adult poems, and they were especially important to the seven-to-nine year olds. The fifth- and sixth-graders were usually somewhat more responsive to the texture and detail of the poems, or at least better able to transfer certain qualities of phrasing and tone to their own work, as in these lines from the sixth-grade Blake poems: "Oh butterfly oh butterfly / Where did you get your burning red wings? . . ." (Lisa Smalley), "When the stars fall to the earth and the purple moon comes out no more . . ." (Andrew Vecchione). Third- and fourth-graders, however, showed they were quite able to get the essentials: "Oh, you must come from a hairy god! . . ." (from "Monkey" by Michelle Woods); ". . . Ant, the most precious, where did you get your body? / Beautiful butterfly, where did you get your wings? . . ." (Arlene Wong).

One thing I think all of my classes profited from was the fact that the children had written a number of their own poems before, independently of the study of the adult works. Some had as many as twenty classes in writing poetry, some only five or six. All had enough to make them feel like poets, however, and this was a great help to them in reading what other poets had written. They were close to poetry because it was something they created themselves. Adult poetry wasn't so strange to them; they could come to it to some degree as equals. A good teacher can bring poetry close to children anyway, but their already feeling easy and happy about it is a real advantage. When they took up their pencils to write works inspired by Blake, Donne, and the other poets, they already knew what it was like to write poetry. They had experience of using comparisons, noises, colors, dream materials, wishes, lies, and so on. This gave them a better chance to create something original in the presence of the adult poems, which might otherwise have been simply too intimidating. I suggest beginning the teaching of poetry with writing alone; then, after five or six lessons, introducing such adult poems as the children seem ready for. In these first classes a teacher can get a sense of what children like about poetry and how best to help them to write and to enjoy it.

In the first few lessons using adult poetry, it may be good to bring it in mainly simply as an inspiration for the children's own work—that is, not discussing the adult poem at all, but merely using it as an example—as I did with the poems by Lawrence and Ashbery. In this way the children can get accustomed to a free and easy relationship with it. One may decide, too, to alternate the classes using adult poetry with some sessions of only writing. The important thing is to keep the atmosphere free, airy, and creative, never weighed down by the adult poems. Once they are too grand and remote, their grandeur and remoteness will be all they communicate; and children, in the classroom as elsewhere, thrive on familiarity, nearness, and affection, and on being able to do something themselves. What matters for the present is not that the children admire Blake and his achievement, but that each child be able to find a tyger of his own.

Of course they can learn more about poetry later, and they will do it better for having read poetry this way now. Even beginning this kind of study in high school, it is not too late to establish the necessary relation between what is in the poems and what is in the student's own mind and feelings and capacity to create for himself. There are of course, special problems with adolescent students—shyness, literariness of some who write, aggression and contempt of some who won't—but a teacher who knows students that age and can be enthusiastic and at the same time free and easy with them about poetry should be able to teach it very well.

There are some extensions and embellishments of this way of teaching that can be tried in elementary school—spending a few weeks on Blake, for example, with every student writing several poems in some way suggested by him and putting together a book of them with illustrations, like Blake's *Songs of Innocence and Experience;* or reading a number of poems which talk to nature in different ways; or reading the work of different poets who lived at the same time. The thing to aim for always, however, is the individual student responding to the individual poem in his own way.

The chapters that follow give details about ten classes on adult poems; how I explained the poems, how the children reacted to the poems, the poetry idea I gave them, and what the poems they wrote were like. This explanatory part of each chapter is followed by a selection of the children's poems. Not all of these are from PS 61. I corresponded with a few teachers elsewhere, whom I knew to be teaching writing, and asked them to try out Blake or Stevens or Shakespeare on their classes. So there are poems influenced by these poets from schools in New Orleans and North Dartmouth, Massachusetts. There are others written by ninth-grade students taught by an American Peace Corps worker at a missionary school in Swaziland, in Africa. I also taught a few classes in secondary schools, and there are poems here by tenth-grade students at the Lycée Français in New York, written in French and English in conjunction with the study of Rimbaud's poem "Voyelles." These poems from different schools show what some students found in the adult poems with the help of the discussion and the poetry idea, and what they were able to do with what they found. A teacher can get from them a rough idea of what to expect. Not that the results of any combination of teacher, children, and adult poetry are predictable—what the children write will vary according to all three. But a good and enthusiastic response to the adult poems does seem a common factor of all these works by children of different ages, in different schools, with different teachers, and even, in the case of the Swazi poems, from different cultures.

Some of the children's poems may be good to use in teaching the adult poems they were written with—to give students confidence by showing them what other children did, to stir up their feelings of emulation, to help them get ideas. Chip's line about Carmen might be just the thing to show some dreamy eleven-year-old his connection with Blake and with ideas of cosmic transformation and to get him started feeling, thinking, and writing.

I'll Carry You Off to Sing with the Train, Maria

Teaching Poetry to Children in Other Countries

After my experience of teaching children to write poetry here in the United States, I did the same kind of teaching in other countries and in other languages—in Haiti, France, Italy, and China. I did the foreign teaching, I think, mostly out of curiosity: to see if the teaching would work, and to see what kinds of poems the children would write. I didn't think that the ease, excitement, and spontaneity, the quick and poetic responsiveness of my students at PS 61 in New York were exclusively American phenomena. I wasn't sure, though, that the kind of teaching I had done at PS 61 could inspire children to write poetry in other countries, with other languages, and with their own highly developed literary and artistic traditions. I found that it could. Taught in much the same way as the children in New York, my students in Port-au-Prince, Paris, Rome, Shanghai, and Beijing responded enthusiastically, understood poems, and wrote well themselves.

The differences in how these different children wrote were less obvious than the similarities. The French children were a little more sophisticated, ironic, and literary—but not much more—than the others; the Italian children somewhat more open, unembarrassed by strong feelings. The Haitian students, once they got going, were vivacious, playful, and a little wild. My American students were perhaps the best at being "crazy," at following fantastic ideas out to the end. The

---

From *Rose, Where Did You Get That Red?* (Vintage, 2d ed., 1990).

Chinese children had a way of their own of mixing the fantastic with the plain and practical: cars on a road looked like a dragon; wishing to go to the moon (a characteristic wish of my American students) became a wish for the moon to come to one's house.

Such differences as there were in part depended on the particular children of a country I happened to be able to teach: for example, the École Alsacienne students in Paris were literally sophisticated in a way that the children at the Genzano school outside Rome were not, quite apart from their being French or Italian. My relative knowledge or ignorance of the children's language was also a factor. My French is pretty good, my Italian is shaky, and, knowing no Chinese, I taught with an interpreter there. Each diminution of my knowledge of the language brought with it a lessening of nuance and perhaps even of imaginativeness in what I was able to help inspire the children to write. Another factor was the length of time I taught: in France, as in Italy, for about two months; in Haiti for only a week; in China for two weeks. In France and Italy, I had time to try out an idea in one class, then use it more effectively in another. Or what children wrote in one class could give me an idea for another poem, another lesson, to give to another class. In Haiti and in China, whatever results I got I had to get quickly; there wasn't much time to try things out. Despite these differences, the remarkable similarity is that all these children liked writing poetry and wrote it well. The ease, excitement, spontaneity, and responsiveness I had been immersed in at PS 61 were all around me, also, in the classrooms of Beijing, Paris, Rome, Port-au-Prince, and Shanghai.

The idea of writing poetry in school, expressing feelings and sensations, and having fun doing it is at least a familiar and respectable one in America, even if it is not often put into effect. Not so in the other countries I taught in, and this unfamiliarity was an obstacle of sorts. The problems it caused were not with the children but with teachers, who were skeptical of what I could accomplish, and of administrators who didn't want to let me try. As soon as I did manage to get into a school, the children were won over; and, in every case, teachers and administrators were themselves won over by what the children wrote. Teachers at the École Bilingue were very skeptical: *Cela ne marchera jamais.* Two of them ended up teaching poetry classes themselves. This was characteristic of what happened. In China and in Italy, teachers I worked with taught poetry while I was there and afterward. They all did it well, strange as it was in the schools where they taught. I wasn't surprised that the teaching worked, but I was surprised by how well it worked. Despite apparent difficulties, poetry seemed to reach the children, to move their imaginations, as directly as bright colors or a spring breeze.

I sometimes began with easy *Wishes, Lies, and Dreams* kinds of lessons, such as a Wish Poem or a Lie Poem, but mostly I used lessons like those in *Rose, Where Did You Get That Red?:* I read aloud and talked about a great poem, then asked children to write poems of their own in some way like it. Most often, I used as models poems in the children's own language: poems by Baudelaire, Rimbaud, Breton, for example, in France; by Dante and Petrarch in Italy; by Li Bai (Li Po) in China. As at PS 61, I paid no attention to whether or not the poems I used were considered suitable for children of this or that age. If something strong and simple in the poem appealed to me, I assumed I could teach it. Here is a brief account of what happened in each country.

My overseas teaching began in 1975 in Haiti, where, at the invitation of the American ambassador, I taught poetry writing for one week at the Lycée Toussaint-L'Ouverture in Port-au-Prince. Though my stay there was short, the vigor, energy, and talent with which the Haitian students responded was impressive. Also impressive was the swiftness with which this lively response came, after a beginning that seemed full of problems. In the first place, not only was I teaching (for the first time) in a language not my own, but also it was not really the language of the students. At home and on the street they spoke Creole; French was a language they learned at school. Thus, when I asked if I could teach ten-year-old students, the minister of education said, "No, they wouldn't be able to write well enough." I was given, instead, students aged fourteen to sixteen. These older children had had time to learn more

French. Furthermore, no one had written poems in school. The French system of education was, if anything, even stricter in Port-au-Prince than it was in France. You were in school to learn and to do this and this and this—not that. In the halls of the *lycée* a man walked back and forth holding a whip. An education official told me, "Oh he never uses it"—but all the same. My Haitian students, at the start, were fearful, puzzled, and hesitant to speak. By the second or third class, though, poetry found them and they found poetry, and difficulties disappeared. By the fifth and last class I had been given an assistant who had the children writing poetry in Creole; they recited, and some even sang, these poems in front of the class. Among the poems I taught were Blake's "Tyger" and Rimbaud's "Vowels." Here is a Blake-inspired poem, with what seem to me some characteristic Haitian surprises, such as the calm mélange of the domestic and the magical and the inclusion of one line in Creole (I've translated the French lines but left the Creole line in the original):

> Little cat what's going on that you're drinking the dog's milk
> My eyes why aren't you looking at me
> My hands why don't you have twenty-five fingers
> Quardrumane why are you so good-looking
> Monsieur Moulongue pou ka ça ou vole conca tout—e tan oua-p vole poul moun-yo
> Tomtom why do you like to beat like that "I am poor I need help"

These are some lines from a lesson on Rimbaud:

> B is black because I am in love with a black girl named Babeth and every time I write the letter B I see it black . . .
> A is white because it looks like a house not painted yet . . .

I taught in France after Haiti, during the winter and spring of 1975–76. I had classes in two prestigious private schools in Paris—the École Bilingue and the École Alsacienne—and in two public schools in the primarily working-class Paris suburb of Petit Clamart. My eighth-grade students at the École Bilingue had sophisticated responses to Rimbaud's "Vowels":

I green like the stems of pale flowers
O yellow like a lemon on a plate
U white like the *Pastilles Vichy* in the subway . . .

E blue as the city on a starry night . . .

The number One is white like an old teapot
Two is violet like a very big drawing
Three is black like the moon hidden by the sun
Four is brown like blond hair . . .

To my sixth-grade students at the École du pavé blanc in Petit Clamart I taught Baudelaire's "L'Invitation au Voyage," an invitation to the poet's beloved to travel with him to a country that is as beautiful, warm, and sensuous as she is— "My child, my sister / Think of how sweet it will be / To go out there and live together / In the country that is like you . . . / There, everything is beauty / Luxury, calm, and voluptuousness . . ." My younger French students had shown an interest in such voyages in writing Wish Poems—

I'd like to live on the sun with Nathalie . . .
I'd like to live in the comic-strip world . . .

The example of Baudelaire inspired strange, dreamy, sensuous, detailed versions of such wishes:

Mother I want you to come with me to that country where all
is so mysterious and so magnificent
And there are those exotic fruits that grow on the hill, hiding
the setting sun that is red as a ruby reflecting in the big
wall mirror that you put up to keep death from coming to
take us away . . .

You'll have flowers in your hair, dresses with long trains, long
as the wind that blows from the north
You'll see volcanoes talking to you about their mysterious
adventure . . .

I taught an "I Never Told Anybody" lesson (a poem of secrets) to the sixth-grade students at the École Bilingue and to the seventh-grade students at the École du pavé blanc. The idea is to put in each line something you've done or thought or felt but never said. I used two different poems in teaching it—Rimbaud's "Dawn" (about a magical morning walk) at the École Bilingue and Mallarmé's "Apparition" (about a mysterious nighttime dream-like vision) at the École du pavé blanc. "Dawn" inspired confessions of feelings about nature; "Apparition," of feelings about the night and dreams—

> I never told anyone that I discovered the language of my
>   fishes
> I never told anyone that a flower gave me one of its petals . . .
>
> I've never said that I talked to the wind . . .
> And I've never said I have a talking flower . . .
> I've never said that I was the ocean
> I've never said that I have a secret in the ocean.
>
> (École Bilingue)
>
> I never told anyone that I believed that in the evening a
>   horseman dressed all in black put up the night
> I never told anyone I believed that in the morning a
>   horseman dressed all in white put up the day . . .
> I never told anyone I dreamed that an angel came to rock me
>   to sleep . . .
>
> (École du pavé blanc)

I used Rimbaud's "Cities" (". . . Houses of crystal and wood that move on invisible rails and pulleys . . . The hunting of bells cries out in the gorges . . .") to inspire poems about an Ideal City. The children wrote: ". . . I live in a city where everything is yellow in the morning / Orange at noon, and red in the evening. / There are no cars in that city. / Everybody walks around in a bathing suit"; ". . . my house [is] filled with wild animals and trees." I used André Breton's poem "The Egret" as a model for an "If only" poem. Breton's poem is full of wishes for the impossible—it begins "If only the sun were shining tonight." My students, like Breton, put an impossible wish in every line—

> If only the radiators were as cold as a photograph
> If only I wrote as well as a lamp that lights up a red leaf like
>   saliva

Another poem by Breton, "Free Union," has some fantastic praise of a woman in every line ("My wife with shoulders of champagne / . . . With fingers of new-cut hay . . ."). I asked my seventh-grade students to praise someone or something that way:

> My dog of snow, of fire and of air,
> My dog of foam, of sparks and of rock,
> My dog of diamond, my dog of ruby,
> My dog green with hope and pink with affection

One remarkable poem was about a door:

> My door of glass which is made of sand and of dust
> My door of vegetable glass which is transparent . . .
> My brilliant door of glass where the moon and the stars are
>   reflected
> My door of glass which encloses the wall of the past
> My door of glass which saw the world born . . .
> My door of glass which will see the world die
> My door of glass which was dead before it was born.

Encouraged by what happened in France, I managed to find a way, two years later, to teach in Italy. I taught in three schools on the outskirts of Rome for several months. In France I had used nineteenth- and twentieth-century poems, those being the ones I knew best; in Italy, for similar reasons, I used mostly Renaissance and earlier poems (Petrarch, Dante, Angiolieri, Cavalcanti) but not entirely (also Leopardi and Marinetti). I used Petrarch's sestina "To Every Animal That Lives on Earth" to inspire sestinas. Dante's "Guido vorrei" (which begins "Guido, I wish that you and Lapo and I / Were carried off by magic / And put in a boat, which, every time there was wind, / Would sail on the ocean exactly where we wanted . . .") seemed a wonderful poem to teach to ten-year-old Italian children. Though it has mysteries for scholars, its main idea is engagingly simple: "Friend, I wish we had a magic vehicle that would take us anywhere we wanted and where we could do as we wish." I asked the children to use names in their poems, as Dante uses the names of his friends

Guido and Lapo, in making their wishful invitations. Some of these had the sweetness and restraint of the original—

> Cynthia, Luigi, Rosalba
> I would like you to come with me
> To travel around the earth on a white and blue ship

Others had mostly its intensity:

> I'd like to take you on a train, Maria
> I'd like to take you to Rome on a train, Maria
> I'd like to sleep on the train, Maria
> I'd like to take you with the train to Venice, Maria
> I'll carry you off to sing with the train, Maria
> I'll give you a kiss on the train, Maria
> I'd like to shoot you with a pistol on the train, Maria
> I'll kill you on the train, Maria
> I'll marry you on the train, Maria

I taught a poem by the twelfth-century poet, Cecco Angiolieri, an extremely aggressive sonnet in which most of the lines begin "Se fossi" (If I were)—"If I were fire, I'd burn up the world / If I were the wind, I'd blow it away . . ." My Genzano students were happy to join in the destruction:

> If I were a window I'd throw my teachers out of me
> If I were a crane, I'd demolish the school
> If I were a panther, I'd bite President Leone . . .

I taught Cavalcanti's poem "Perch'i' no spero," which begins "Because I do not hope ever to return / Little song of mine, to Tuscany / Go you, lightly and softly / Straight to my lady . . ." Once it is there, Cavalcanti wants his poem to talk to his lady about him. I asked my students to write a poem addressed to their poem itself, asking it to do something for them, anything at all. The results were, sometimes, like Cavalcanti's poem, full of strong feeling:

> Oh my poem
> Go and speak of me
> To my ancestors and to everyone I know

Speak of my kind teacher
Good like a father
Oh my beautiful poem say to all
That the world is more beautiful, if the
People are kind
Go, I pray you
I, it is obvious, can't visit the world
Go, you are my only hope.

There was something in Leopardi's poetry I thought I could teach to children, but it took me a while to find it. There seemed to be no helpfully imitatable form in poems like "La Luna" and "L'Infinito" but there was the strong presence of a feeling I thought the children would respond to: loneliness, solitude. For the Leopardi class, I read "La Luna" and "L'Infinito" aloud, explained what was difficult in them, and talked about their atmosphere of loneliness. I asked for poems about times of being or feeling alone. For form I suggested beginning every line with the world *alone* (*solo* or *sola*).

Alone the bird flies in the month of September
Alone with a girl in a car in the dark
Alone in my room thinking of my little dog who died
Alone I was studying one summer morning . . .

. . . I was alone in the country
I was alone in the mountains
I was alone in a boat
I was alone in class

I taught Marinetti's "To a Racing Car" (it begins "Vehement god of a race of steel, / Automobile drunk on space . . .") somewhat as I had taught Breton's "Free Union," to inspire a poem of exaggerated praise or boasting:

My piano, when I want it to, turns into the ocean, the
    universe, the mountains . . .

My car runs not on gas but on gold
My car moves faster than light
My car cries because I go to school
My car has a blue fiancée . . .

My Italian students openly expressed their enthusiasm for their new subject—

> Don't worry, Poetry,
> I'll never abandon you
> Even if when I grow up
> I forget about you
> I beg you, make me remember
> Of you, the beautiful thoughts that I had
> When I knew you . . .
>
> Poetry you seem a person dressed in white in the middle of
> many people dressed in blue I know you right away . . .

Teaching in China was my most ambitious endeavor, since I didn't know the language and I had very little idea of what Chinese education, or Chinese school children, were like. (I was invited to China to read and lecture in 1984 by the Writers Union. Teaching in schools was something that was worked out after I got there.) I taught six lessons in Beijing and four in Shanghai. In Beijing I taught with Zhu Ciliu, a professor and poet, who was perfectly bilingual. Facing the two hundred children the Chinese authorities had given me as students, I would speak for a minute or two—explaining the poetry ideas, giving suggestions—then turn to Zhu Ciliu who would translate for the children what I had said. Timidity and unsureness led me to use simple poetry ideas like Wishes and I-used-to-but-now for my first six lessons. In China I really didn't know if the teaching was going to work at all. The children, however, sitting there, being told through an interpreter to write poems, which I don't believe they had ever done in school (certainly not this way), were at first puzzled, then quickly excited. They wrote, covering their notebook pages with Chinese characters, at what seemed to me an incredible pace:

> I wish I had a box in which there was everything . . .
>
> I wish Newton had not been born yet so the law of gravity
> would be my discovery
> I wish summer would last forever so I wouldn't have to say
> good-bye to my beautiful skirt with flowers on it . . .

I was very very fat, too fat to walk
Now I am very very thin, like a bamboo . . .

These first lessons having gone well, I felt bold enough—with a great deal of help from Zhu Ciliu—to use some classic Chinese poems as models. Zhu Ciliu suggested this quatrain by the eighth-century poet Liu Yongyuan, which describes a scene partly by saying what is not there:

No birds flying over the hills
No one on the mountain trails
Only a fisherman in palm cape and straw hat
Fishing alone on a river in falling snow.

In the original, the first two lines begin with the word MEIYO, "there is not." The poem was read aloud and written on the blackboard. I asked the children to begin their first two or three lines with MEIYO and then conclude with a word like *only* to say what *was* there. Each line of Liu Yongyuan's poem has seven Chinese characters. I told the children they could if they liked make their lines of seven characters, too:

There is no green grass
There are no sweet-smelling flowers
Over the blurry barren hill
There is only flying snow

No one walking on the path
No bird flying in the trees
Only one person on a bench
Reading out loud in a foreign language

Another class was based on some lines by Li Bai about the Yellow River:

The Yellow River with its water from the sky
Flows on and on into the sea . . .
Bursting through the Kunlun Mountain in the West
The Yellow River roars across ten thousand li and leaps over
    the Dragon Gate

I told the children to imagine they were looking at something that was very long and that came from far away—like a river, a mountain range, the sky—and to write a poem about where it began, where it went, and where it ended:

> A gust of hard wind from the Yangtse River
> Raising up flying sand blowing moving stones
> Ranging as if in a land with no people
> Roaring roaring until it stops at the Huang Po

> Shan Yin Street comes from the sky
> Deep and long it leads to the earth
> The stream of cars runs without end
> Like a huge dragon it rolls to a distant place.

The best poetry, it turned out, was as inspiring to children in China, Haiti, Italy, and France as it had been to my students in New York. French children were moved by Baudelaire to create landscapes that mirrored their feelings; Italian children, following Dante and Cecco, to propose ideal voyages and to create vigorous invective; Chinese ten-year-olds found mysterious solitudes in present-day Shanghai as Liu Yongyuan had found them in the eighth-century countryside. No matter how much I had expected, these results were surprising, suggesting, as they did, the probable universality of the power—still, sadly, by so many, unrecognized—of children's imagination and intelligence.

Quiet

What follows is a chapter from a book on teaching old and ill
people in a nursing home to write poetry. I did this work with
poet Kate Farrell. Most of our students were unable to write
because of physical problems so we had them dictate their
poems to us. I began by explaining the "poetry idea" and after-
wards read the students' poems aloud. This "Quietness" chap-
ter is a good illustration of what the lessons were like.

The poetry idea was Write a poem about the quietest times,
or the quietest things, you can think of. You can mention
different kinds of quietness in every line or so, or you can
make the whole poem about one thing.

I read aloud some poems to give ideas as to how quietness
was part of poetry and to suggest various kinds of quietness:
the quietness of a scene one sees, the quiet of a room, the
quiet of being with people when no one speaks. And the
quiet of nature, and the silence one may feel in the presence
of something that seems beautiful or important. The poems
I read that speak of these kinds of quiet are all short, and I
had time to talk about each one: D. H. Lawrence's "The
White Horse," William Carlos Williams's "Nantucket," and a
haiku by Ryota. This was the first time I read others' poems
to the class. I was happy to see how much they got from
them. "The White Horse" and the Ryota poem, in particular,
seemed to influence both the mood and the music of our
students' work.

From *I Never Told Anybody: Teaching Poetry Writing in a Nursing Home*
(Random House, 1977).

The White Horse

The youth walks up to the white horse, to put its halter on
and the horse looks at him in silence.
They are so silent they are in another world.

Lawrence's poem suggests a way to make a poem about one
brief incident and also makes silence seem a sort of magical
thing, at least mysterious. The repeating sounds of *silence* and
silent seem part of what makes the poem so final and quiet.
The haiku is a little list of silent things, with a surprising
conclusion:

No one spoke—
the host, the guests,
the white chrysanthemums.

I read this twice (the students liked it), and along with my
localized version of it (No one spoke— / Kate, Suzanne / the
white chairs) it seemed to help students to make poems of lists
of quiet things. It also, with its strangely silent chrysanthe-
mums, suggested the mystery of a quiet time. Williams's
poem is also mainly a list, of the things in the room of a
Nantucket inn—like the other two short poems, it has a
strong and surprising last line—

Nantucket

Flowers through the window
lavender and yellow

changed by white curtains—
Smell of cleanliness—

Sunshine of late afternoon—
On the glass tray

a glass pitcher, the tumbler
turned down, by which

a key is lying—And the
immaculate white bed

I said, "Here are some poems about quietness by some other poets." I didn't speak of them with reverence nor stress distinctions between their own work and that of the poets I read. This isn't bad for a student's judgment but, rather, helps him to see what is good both in his own work and in that of another poet. If a poem by D. H. Lawrence is of another species from his, he is separated by a barrier of "poetic class" from what a great poet writes; he feels (and, I believe, is) less able to come up to what the other has done. Reading poems aloud to students, of which I did a good deal after this, was the best way to help them know poetic literature, since most had physical problems that made it hard for them to read.

Though the quietness idea suggested strong feelings somewhat more than colors did, it didn't ask for them directly. Quietness seems no more important in itself than colors are. There is no strong position to take. The deep emotions silence is connected to are come on by surprise—emotions of times when one was all alone—feeling happy, peaceful, afraid, or overwhelmed.

Leroy's poem, about the beautiful quiet fishing trip, when he "caught a lot of fish. / All the stars were shining / The ocean was quiet . . ." was dictated quickly and surely. He had found his subject and what he would say before we came to take the poem down. This was unusual in these early classes. Many students hadn't yet separated making up a poem from mere conversation. Hearing someone talk very rapidly and randomly about something, we might stop her, as Kate stopped Mary Tkalec, who was talking this time about how quiet it was in church. Kate said, "Yes, that's right, churches are quiet. How do you want me to write that down in your poem?" Mary said, "You write it down, you can express it better than I can," but Kate said, "No, it's your poem, and I like the way you're telling it to me." And "What should I write down?" When it was clear that what was said was being taken down as a line, the student was more concentrated.

Some students did not ramble, but instead could find nothing to say until we talked to them a little. George Johnson said, "I can't think of anything . . . not today." Sometimes this meant a student really felt too bad to talk, but usually, and especially in the early classes, it meant he lacked confidence and had a false idea of the kind of thing he was being asked for. One has to talk and make the situation clear. Talk about quiet and one's own experience of it, for example. One of George's difficulties was that he tried to think of something with no noise whatsoever and couldn't. Kate was with him and said that indeed everything did have some noise and that quiet was probably a matter of contrast; she remembered the quiet of walking home from piano lessons when it was just getting dark. George said, "Yes, that's right." Kate said, "I know everything has some noise, but just remember the quietest thing you can." And he remembered the silence after he "got beaten," that was all, but he was very happy with it when Kate read it back to him and when I read it to the class. The people we taught weren't used to the kind of respectfully determined interest in their imaginings and perceptions that we had. It seems possible they weren't used to being listened to that much at all. So it was understandable that we had, at first, to talk, to convince, to reassure, to explain. The dramatic effect of Sam Rainey's poem was due not only to the poetry idea and the poems I read aloud but also to Kate's continuing to ask for one more quiet time. Encouraged to go on, he wrote about three times in his life he hadn't before thought of as being connected.

Students' Poems

The quietest time I ever remember in my life
Was when they took off my leg.

Another quiet time is when you're with someone you like
And you're making love.

And when I hit the number and won eight hundred dollars
That was quiet, very quiet.

Sam Rainey

Sitting alone in a church is the quietest moment in my life.
It's so quiet that you can hear your breathing.

And your own heart beating.
When you go back home you feel very relieved and happy.

Mary Tkalec

I like to be off by myself.
I never liked a lot of noise.
I was quiet in my childhood, just sitting is quiet.
And nobody around to do a lot of talking.
I used to go off by myself.
Daisies and violets and wild roses are quiet
If I saw them along the road.

Florence Wagner

I always was quiet
And my mother always had to send my sisters into the room
To see what made me so quiet.

Fred Richardson

I love it when it's quiet.
Lonely hour in the night it's so quiet
That often I think of things when I was a child.
I think of things my grandmother taught me.
To be honest, thoughtful and to love everybody.
Never to hold malice.

Mary L. Jackson

Mary Zahorjko.
A quiet name.

Mary Zahorjko

When I was a little boy and got beaten
It was quiet afterwards.

George Johnson

I used to be off by myself.
Anything that doesn't answer you back is quiet.
Clocks, watches, anything.
I repaired them
And put them together and that was it.

Harry Siegel

Plowboy

The quietest thing in my life was after plowing acres of
    corn
Then overlooking the work I did and seeing if my row
    was straight.
I was up on the hill with nobody but me then
And no birds making a sound.
Usually after plowing, crows come and pluck the seeds
    out of the ground.
But this time there were no crows.

William Ross

The quietest night I remember
Was going out deep-sea fishing.
Me and my friend were way out on a rowboat fishing.
We caught a lot of fish.
All the stars were shining
The ocean was quiet
The wind was quiet
And we were quiet.
And the fish were biting.

Leroy Burton

IV

Educating the Imagination

When I first thought of teaching poetry, which I did to adults at the New School a long time ago, I knew there was a standard kind of poetry workshop in which there are twelve students who write poetry and a teacher, and every week a student has a turn. The poet prints up some poems, and everybody reads them and comments on them. In that kind of workshop you find out how you're doing, how good you are, how publishable you are, and so on. You get the advantages of knowing other poets and getting their criticism, but that seemed to me not enough. I wanted to do something new. I tried to think of a way to bring into the classroom all of the things that I thought had made me inspired to write poems and made me write better, and I figured out a way to do this, which I got better at doing as I went on doing it.

To the question, "What makes a writer better?" obviously, one answer is reading other poets and being influenced by them, so one of the first assignments I had my adult poets do

The transcript of a talk given at the conference *Educating the Imagination II: A Celebration of Kenneth Koch,* held at the Teachers and Writers Collaborative's Center for Imaginative Writing. From *Teachers and Writers Collaborative Newsletter,* 1994.

was to read William Carlos Williams. This was particularly relevant at the time, though I still do it at Columbia, because when I started teaching at the New School, in the early sixties or maybe the fifties even, there were still a number of students whose idea of poetry was something like "O wingéd being soaring through the azure," and Williams can show you quickly the pleasure of saying "Bird there in the blue," or something like that. In other words, the word *woman* is closer to your heart than the word *damsel,* and so on and so forth. Also, Williams writes about ordinary things that are right in front of you. He uses the language that we speak, which had helped me when I read him seriously for the first time, when I was around eighteen years old.

I lived in Cincinnati, Ohio, and my first big influence after nursery rhymes had been Shelley. My uncle Leo, who worked in the family furniture store, had me down to the store one day and took me up to a big safe that was upstairs. At this time, he confessed to me that he had written poems. I was fifteen, and he had written poems when he was nineteen. They were all sonnets, he said, and about some love that was unrequited. He wanted me to see them. He didn't think they were very good, but he also wanted to give me a book. So he gave me his sonnets, and he also gave me a book of the *Complete Poems of Percy Bysshe Shelley.* I remember the *Bysshe* was very important to me, as was the red cover of the book and also the wonderful picture of Shelley with wild hair and an open collar. That, for me, suddenly was poetry, and I wrote a number of poems then, which were influenced by Shelley, but they weren't very much like Shelley. I remember the beginnings of a few. They were sonnets. One began "When young I feared two things, cancer and war." The last line was "I never once had known they were the same." I wrote another one, not exactly based on my experience, which began "And as a growing eaglet." You can imagine I'd seen a lot of eaglets!

> And as a growing eaglet feebly tries
> To spread his new-formed wings and soar through space
> Alas, he cannot leave his nesting place. . . .

It was a Petrarchan sonnet about being fifteen years old, and it ended with the line "Not yet a man, and still no more a child." Well, I did get something from Shelley despite these bad poems I wrote. . . . I know I'm in a vast parenthesis. Just imagine that I'm starting over again.

I think that sometimes one of the first stages of somebody's having a talent for poetry is the use of exaggerated, distant, remote, and fancy language like "And as a growing eaglet feebly tries / To spread his new-formed wings and soar through space." It seems to me that's one way to get away from the world of your parents, your brothers and sisters, the other children on the block. It's a way of playing with poetry. You make yourself happy by saying "infinitesimal." If you say "the infinitesimal sun," it's wonderful. It's not any good, but it's not to be disdained. To disdain it is like going around cutting down the first little green shoots in the garden: you never get any flowers.

When I was teaching at the New School, the things I wanted to bring into the classroom were: reading other poets and being influenced; trying new forms, like sestinas, say, or poems with only one word in each line; collaborating with other poets; writing about dreams; writing stream-of-consciousness; deliberately writing things that didn't make sense; and so on. All these things I turned into assignments, so that every week we weren't talking about how good or bad the students were, but about good ways to write about dreams or good ways to get meaning into one word in a one-word line. It worked very well, and I've been doing it ever since at Columbia.

When I went into PS 61 to teach, I thought I'd do the same things, but I found that I couldn't, for various reasons. I couldn't get the children to read William Carlos Williams and Ezra Pound and be influenced by them. I found that there were all kinds of things I couldn't get the children to do.

As for trying difficult forms, this was all pulverized into one form or variations of one form: repetition. I would say, "Start every line with 'I wish,' " "Put your favorite color in every line," "Start the first line with 'I used to' and the second line with 'But now,' " and so on. It was a children's version of what I had done with adults.

Some people criticized my method—especially at first, though there are still critics of it—saying that, well, children are so spontaneous, they're just naturally poets. This is sort of like saying that people are naturally good cooks. I don't know if anybody is naturally a poet, but children are spontaneous, and they say interesting things. The critics asked, "Why are you interfering with their spontaneity by telling them what to write about?" The reason, of course, is that I may be inspired to write a poem by walking past a bakery, listening to music, falling in love, or reading a poem, but none of this happens to anyone at nine o'clock in the morning at PS 61. You have to make something like it happen there. Actually, if I asked you all to write a poem, probably the hardest thing for all of you would be what to write about, unless you'd been writing all day. I gave children assignments to inspire them, not to limit them. I said, "Start every line with 'I wish,'" not "Start every line with 'I am grateful for.'" My assignments are meant to be used, as all the teachers who have used them successfully know, just to get things started, to help children to write *poems* instead of just talking about what they feel. When you write a poem, it's as if you are saying how you feel on a grid, and you are hanging flowers everywhere on it.

As for the assignments that I dreamed up, I hadn't intended them to be just formulas. My ideas came from my particular experience as to what inspired me, and I don't think there would be much more agreement on what you would have in a poetry writing class than there would be on what you would have in a domestic science class. In both you have to bring in things, but different things for different kinds of cooking and different kinds of poetry.

I thought that it would be worthwhile to go over in some detail the things and the poets that have influenced me, helped me to write, made me write better than I would have otherwise. I'm going to go into a little more detail than I did just now. One effect of this might be to encourage other poets who teach in schools to think about their own experiences and, thus, to find in them some ideas for teaching, and I thought maybe it would have some interest even if it did not accomplish that. This is not an organized speech: it will be anecdotal and autobiographical. Remember that the general idea is things that excited me about writing poetry and how I learned them and who influenced me and so on. You're supposed to think the same things about yourself, you're not supposed to be interested so much in what happened to me.

The first page of my notes has on top of it in big letters THE ESCAPE. I was brought up in Cincinnati, Ohio. My parents were very nice. The first time I wrote a poem, my mother gave me a big kiss and said, "I love you." The whole idea of writing poetry had a lot to do with escaping, escaping from the bourgeois society of Cincinnati, Ohio, escaping from any society of Cincinnati, Ohio, and escaping from any society anywhere. The first thing I had to find out to be a poet at all was that there was a bigger world, a bigger world than that of my school and my parents and their friends. I had to find out that there was a world where people talked to the moon or said, "O wild west wind," that there was a past that was even more exhilarating and interesting than the Egypt and Ethiopia that I studied in fourth-grade geography.

Then, I had to find out that there was a bigger language than the one that I spoke and my friends and parents spoke. Instead of "Oh, there's the most darling blouse down at Altman's. Let's go down there tomorrow," I had to find out that you could say, "O wild West Wind, thou breath of Autumn's being." I had to find out you could say, "Let me not to the marriage of true minds admit impediment." In saying so, I was lifted way above all these troubles of Cincinnati, Ohio, these troubles that seemed to be suffocating me though I had a relatively happy childhood. I had to find this big language with words like "impediment" and "wild west wind" and the idea of talking to everything. Then, I had to find some bigger poetic forms than I knew about, bigger poetic forms than nursery rhymes. I had to find sonnets, odes, and things like that. That was the first stage.

No sooner had I found all of these things than I had to start getting rid of them. I was writing corny poetry like "When young I feared two things, cancer and war" or "And as a growing eaglet feebly tries." No sooner had I found these things that made me a poet—the bigger subject matter, the bigger language, the bigger forms—than I had to find which forms and diction were right for me and which big subjects were right for me to talk about. One I found was my feelings about my girlfriends. That was a good one to talk about. Another was the pleasure I got driving in a car, because I started driving a car, as all the idiotic teenagers did, at about fourteen. It was a crazy law that allowed me to drive. Driving in my car and walking my dog were good subjects for me. Talking to the west wind was not a good subject for me. I didn't know what the west wind was. I found that sonnets weren't good for me, but certain forms were. Mainly free verse was good for me with, sometimes, a little rhyme.

Once I'd found this, then I had to get rid of all of that because I was writing like Kenneth Patchen or I was writing like e. e. cummings or I was writing like Williams. I had to do something new, and that was very hard. It seems that when I went into the schools to teach children, I was skipping the first parts; that is, I was skipping the part of the bigger world, the bigger language, and the bigger forms. I was going right into the classroom with poets who might inspire the children to find something new of their own. That's what I wanted to do. This seemed to work all right. Once I found this way of writing modern poetry, I had to get rid of that because I didn't want to sound like Eliot and Pound and Williams. Ever since then, I've had to try to write poems not like the ones I wrote before. It's an unending process, so one can have a poetry teacher forever. In this case it's largely oneself.

It's wonderful to get children to start to write because it makes them happy, as I say in *Wishes, Lies, and Dreams*. It gives them self-confidence. It makes them like to read books. I had students who actually started coming to school with books! I also noticed that when I stopped teaching at the school—or when Ron Padgett, who succeeded me, stopped—the children stopped writing poetry. If you want people to go on having the pleasure of writing poetry, along with the attendant dangers, the best thing you can do for them is to get them to read. If you can somehow get them to like reading poetry, then they can go on being their own poetry teachers, and if they like to write, they can go through all these phases. But if they don't read, it probably won't happen.

Among the things I needed to escape from at various times were rhyme and meter. In fact, I had to escape from not being able to rhyme, then I had to escape from rhyme. Poetry is like trying a lot of clothes you eventually have to get rid of. I had to escape from rhyme and meter, and anybody who helped me to do that I admired a lot, such as William Carlos Williams and Walt Whitman. I was hungry. By the time I was seventeen or eighteen years old, I was just crazy with a thirst to find poetry that didn't rhyme and that didn't use meter. I was so grateful to anybody who didn't do it. I liked practically everybody who wrote in free verse.

Then, I needed people to help me get away from making sense in the usual way, because if you make sense in the usual way, it's like an asymptote, the thing in mathematics that gets close to a line but never gets all the way to it. You never escape from the rabbi and your parents and your teacher if you go on making sense in the usual way because they're all making sense in the usual way, and they're older than you are, and they can do it better. So I had to make some other kind of sense. I was very grateful to dada and surrealism and anything crazy. I remember something John Ashbery said to me at Harvard, where we were both students. We were reading each other's poems. He had just read Alfred Jarry, and he said, "Kenneth, I just read somebody named Alfred Jarry." I said, "Well?" I was waiting for the news. I was always waiting for the news. He said, "I think we should be a little crazier." I said, "Yes, yes." I wanted to do that, so I was very glad for anybody who could help me to be crazier. By the way, in a classroom with little children, a good thing I happened to say was "Be crazy, be stupid." I think there are actually people who go into a classroom and say, "Be imaginative." You know, you get gingerbread houses and fairy princesses.

I also needed poets who could show me how to avoid dead seriousness, high seriousness. I grew up in a time when T. S. Eliot was, as Delmore Schwartz said, the literary dictator of the West, and not only were you supposed to be serious, you were supposed to be a little depressed. You could read through the quarterlies—the *Kenyon Review,* the *Partisan Review,* the *Sewanee Review*—all the big journals of those days, and nobody was seeing anything at the end of that tunnel. They were not even seeing the tunnel. I remember being exhilarated when I read Nietzsche. He said you should be very careful how long you look into the abyss because the abyss is also looking into you. I was very grateful to William Carlos Williams because he seemed happy so much of the time. And to the French poet Saint-John Perse, because he looked at the waves rolling in over the ocean and he saw blue enchantresses, kings, mountains, decades—it was wonderful.

I also needed poetry to help me escape my natural prudery, my natural timidity about talking about sex or being crazy or out of line, because when I was seventeen and eighteen years old I was very proud, for all my avant-garditude, of being a nice upper-middle-class boy in Cincinnati. What kind of poetry was that going to result in? I needed poetry to get me away from my ignorance, because although I had a pretty good education, I was very ignorant. Of course, I loved Eliot and Pound. Whether they were really smart or not I didn't know, but they certainly seemed smart. I needed to get away from what was supposedly poetic subject matter. I had a high school teacher, Katherine Lappa, to whom I dedicated *Wishes, Lies, and Dreams,* who really helped me to do that. I needed poetry to get me away from my usual way of talking and writing.

Shakespeare and Shelley were very helpful, Shakespeare because of the lift his iambic pentameter gives to almost anything one says:

> Thou seest Ron Padgett sitting on my right.
> Behind him Anania holds his sway,
> And both with folded hands do listen now
> To what I say to you upon this night.

With Shakespeare, it is like pumping air into everything you say. It goes. It's great. That's something I never tried with children, which, if I went back into schools, I would like to try.

I remember I was very ambitious when I started teaching children. I assumed they could understand anything, so I read them the beginning of *Paradise Lost*:

> Of Mans First disobedience, and the fruit
> Of that Forbidden Tree, whose mortal tast
> Brought Death into the World, and all our woe

and so forth. The children were looking at me. I asked, "What does that sound like?" Some smart child, a fifth grader in the back row, said, "It sounds like the preacher." What else do you get out of it the first time you read it, other than that it sounds like the preacher? I thought that was a good answer. In any case, Shakespeare showed me a way to float anything: "I take this piece of paper in my hand / And read it to you." That's wonderful. Shelley did too. He showed me not only how to make it float, but how to be excited about it. He taught me how to be burning, feverish, vague, hurried, in a great rush. I liked anybody who would do this for me.

Keats was another poet I loved, for his lusciousness and sensuousness. No matter what story is going on in "The Eve of St. Agnes," it's all about the fact that there's a stained-glass window and red light is falling on Madeline's fair breast as she sits praying. That's what seems strongest. And "lucent syrops tinct with cinnamon." Even when they're escaping at the last minute, it's all about the sound of this big iron door opening. It's luscious. I liked Keats's letters too—he says that before he wrote poetry—take that, T. S. Eliot—he cultivated a feeling of deliberate happiness. That was the state in which he could write poetry best. I don't think I was directly influenced by Keats, though he gave me an ideal of lushness and richness and of how much you can get into a poem, how much you can get in every line. It's not just "They are standing on the sidewalk looking at the dump truck." The great thing in the poetry of Frank O'Hara—particularly the early poetry—was that life is so full of a variety of exciting things, exciting people, and exciting ideas that you are just crazy if you're not responding to them. I think Keats, Frank O'Hara, and Gerard

Manley Hopkins were all poets who made me feel that I could get a whole lot of stuff together whether I understood it or not and that I should put as much as possible into every line of every poem.

Whitman was an inspiration because he showed me a way to float things, the way Shakespeare did. "I take this piece of paper in my hand / And read upon it every word": that's Shakespeare. But Whitman taught me another way to float everything:

> I see the piece of paper and I pick it up.
> I look at the piece of paper and I see what's written on it.
> I read the words and they're good words and I'm reading
> them to you.

It's terrific, but what am I saying? The music makes it say something. And there's always a possibility that once you get going in this motorboat, it's going to go somewhere. Also, it really is true about Whitman what the French writer Valery Larbaud said, that the main thing that Whitman showed to twentieth-century American poets was that greatness in poetry can come not from difficulties overcome but from—and this is better in French, *facilités trouvées*—easinesses found. Whitman shows you, why not do what is easy? Why not say, "I lean and loafe at my ease, observing a spear of summer grass" instead of saying, "Beyond the garden wall where. . . ." Just write it the way you would say it. Write about what is right in front of you, what you like. There really aren't any prizes for solving difficulties in poetry. I remember a particularly irritating review of a book of poetry, at a time when nobody would publish my work or Frank's or John's. The reviewer praised it by saying, "Mr. X admirably meets the demands of his forms." Well, isn't that amazing? I'm pretty good at walking sideways, but I don't see anything so great about it.

A poet who inspired me as much as anybody, probably more, is William Carlos Williams, whom I read hard for about three or four months, the way only a baby poet can read somebody. I was nineteen. I started when I was seventeen, but then when I got out of the army, when I was nineteen, I read Williams a lot more. I realized then that I could write about what I was really doing. All these vacant lots in Cincinnati, these suburban houses, the gutters, the automobiles, the schoolyards were things that I could write about. I hadn't known that before. One great thing, of course, that artists do, including poets, is to open up new subject matter. There's a wonderful poem by Paul Éluard. It's called something like "Eighty-seven Words I Have Up Till Now Been Forbidden to Use." It's a poem in which he deliberately puts in eighty or a hundred words that he hasn't been able to use in poems until then. Well, I hadn't been able to use words like *dog, parking lot,* and *sidewalk,* and from Williams I learned that I could.

There are two secret sensual pleasures in Williams. One: it's a lot of fun to write in short lines. It's like flamenco dancing. You don't have a long line that you have to fill up. You say, "I pick up / the piece of paper." Another secret pleasure I got from Williams was the pleasure of interrupting yourself, of hesitating in odd places, which you don't get to do at home or with your friends. They'd think you're stammering or you've gone crazy: "I have eaten / the plums / that were in / the icebox / and which / you were probably / saving / for breakfast." You can even say, "for break / fast" or "a red wheel / barrow." It's nice, it's a lot of fun. It gives one all kinds of new music. Williams, who seemed to be apt to destroy the music of poetry, created a new kind.

Wallace Stevens, I found him very inspiring. I was envious. I couldn't understand how he did certain things. At the end of "Disillusionment of Ten O'clock," there are two lines about an old sailor, who, drunk and asleep, "Catches tigers / In red weather." I couldn't, for the life of me, think of two short lines that had such strong stresses, "Catches tigers / In red weather." Of course they have internal rhyme. Oh, how older people used to torment me talking about internal rhyme! "Stevens has internal rhyme." Internal rhyme you just get naturally. If you give up the rhyme at the end of the line, you find it turning up inside the lines. In any case, "red weather" was obviously an example of internal rhyme, and after a while you figure out the left hand/right hand sort of poetry, the difference between accent and stress, whichever you choose. While one hand is going da-dum da-dum da-dum da-dum, the other is saying, "Put out the light and then put out the light." Some poetry, Stevens's in this case, is completely stressed; that is, there is no meter. It's just the natural stress that you put on words, but I hadn't understood that yet. I had been going through Clement Wood's rhyming dictionary. The last forty pages are devoted to poetic forms, and I had been going through them writing ballades, ballades royales, and things like that. If you write in meter, you don't ever get anything like "Catches tigers / In red weather." That's one thing I admired.

I also admired the way he could be so flat and so elegant at the same time:

> A man and a woman
> Are one.

I tried to do it myself:

> My dog and I
> Are one.
> My dog and I and the chimney
> Are one.

No, it didn't work. People who don't write poetry might not know how many months one could spend trying to write something like "A man and a woman and a blackbird are one" and have it sound like poetry. Anyway, that was very interesting. Things like:

> I was of three minds,

That's also very hard to do.

Also, I loved the way he told stories sometimes, elegant, gorgeous stories that to me didn't make any sense, as in his "Anecdote of the Prince of Peacocks," a great poem, which so far as I know doesn't make sense in any ordinary way.

He says that the blue ground "Was full of blocks / And blocking steel." It sounds as though it means something, but I don't know what it means. It means what it is. I tell my students in college, "If you don't know what this means, just respond to it as if it were a story: once there was a blue ground, and it was full of blocks. Then you'll understand it. There was a blue ground, and it was full of blocks." I like that kind of narrative. Stevens, in a poem like that and in a number of others, it seems to me, is creating modern fairy tales, legends in the same way that, in painting, Paul Klee did, Miro did, and Max Ernst did. I was endlessly intrigued by that little Max Ernst of the two children frightened by a nightingale. I found no way to figure it out. I love certain Picasso works for the same reason, that they seem to be telling a very moving, a very important story, but you don't know exactly what the story is about.

I liked almost all dada and surrealist art at first and a lot of Picasso. I liked Matisse because of the sensuousness of it, and I was inspired by a remark that Matisse made. I thought maybe I wrote poems that way. He said, "The way I make paintings is I have a white canvas and I put a splash of pink on it, and then, with every succeeding stroke, I try to keep the canvas as beautiful as it was with just that one stroke of pink." That's asking a lot of a poem, but we might as well try it. All of these things, I think, can be brought into the classroom; that is, they would be things that I would try, but everybody has his own experiences.

I was also inspired by tapestries, frescoes, and predellas, anything that tells a story that you can't quite figure out. I guess if I were a devout Christian, I could have figured out the tapestries and the frescoes a little better than I was able to, but I would see in one tapestry somebody tearing off his clothes and in another somebody holding up a sheep. I really liked this because of the beauty of the detail and because it was telling a story, but I didn't know the story.

I liked other poets for other reasons. I loved Max Jacob because he was able to be sensuous and mysterious at the same time he was funny. When I first read Frank O'Hara's poetry, I was moved by the fact that he used a lot of exclamation marks. This seems a small thing, but I hadn't had exclamation marks in my poetry before. Kate Farrell and I taught old people in a nursing home—we wrote about it in a book called *I Never Told Anybody*—and the second or third time, Kate and I had the old people write using comparisons. We realized that in the first few poems people had written, there hadn't been a single comparison. In my poetry, when I was about twenty years old, there hadn't yet been any exclamations or invocations "O this! O that!"

Another inspiring thing about Frank's work I got from his poem called "Today." In it he mentions aspirin tablets, jujubes, and sequins, all tiny things with perfect shapes. My poetry got filled with tiny things like yo-yos and marbles. Before that, I had just been writing about big things. I remember, I graduated from Harvard before John and Frank did. I had known John when I was there. I hadn't known Frank. John sent me some of Frank's poems and he said, "I think there's another contender here." I read Frank's poems, which were all about jujubes and marbles, yo-yos, and televisions, and I wrote back and said, "I don't think he's as good as we are." I took these poems to Europe with me. I had a Fulbright grant that year, and I read them on the train to Vienna. Then I suddenly got illuminated. Frank dedicated his book to me, "To Kenneth and the Vienna illumination."

Someone wrote that I helped make poetry easier to understand. I don't know. Apollinaire said about his friends the cubist painters that they were tearing down the world so it could be put together properly. It seemed to me that what I was doing and what my friends were doing in poetry was to get rid of the old, fat referential difficulty in order to break everything down into splashes, dots, and cubes and put it back together in an interesting way. I don't think I was making poetry easy and accessible when I wrote that, but I certainly wasn't trying to make it more difficult—just truer to what I thought, then it ought to be.

> And, dame! kong swimming with my bets,
> Aladdin, business, out Chanukah of May bust

Sit rumors of aethereal business coo-hill-green
Diamonds, moderns modesty. "There sit
The true of two hens of out-we-do maiden
Monastery belongs to (as! of!) can tip up off cities
Ware fizzle dazzle clothes belong. . . ."

(from When the Sun Tries to Go On)

Collaborating with Painters

The first collaboration I did with a painter was with Larry Rivers, in his studio, in 1961. We worked together, with oil paint, pastel, pen, pencil, and charcoal, directly on paper and canvas. We did a series of maps, a series about women's shoes, and some more or less "abstract" works. Finally we did a large painting/poem called *New York 1950–1960*. I remember being pretty excited. Not only was collaborating a way to be at work and at a party at the same time, but it gave me the chance to do a kind of work I couldn't otherwise do. I had an instantaneous perceptive audience for every move I made (word I wrote); ordinarily getting a response takes longer than that. We worked fast, and wanted to get a lot done. If my words weren't perfect, Larry could fix them with some red or yellow; the same for his brushstrokes and pictures, I could amend them with adjectives and nouns. At least, we assumed so. All this created an atmosphere, of speed and excitement, that might or might not make for really good work, but it made for a certain kind of work that neither of us did alone, and whatever this was might turn out to be good. There was always a chance, too, that we could in however small a way realize some kind of Rimbaud-like dream of doing more with words and colors than words could ever do alone—of finding the colors of the vowels, saying what couldn't be said. These first collaborations gave me a taste for working with painters that hasn't much changed. I will almost always say yes to the prospect of a collaborative work. The direct collaborating I did with Larry

From *Collaborating with Artists* (catalogue) (Ipswich Museum, England, 1993).

is the kind I like best. I worked somewhat similarly much (thirty years) later with Red Grooms on a series of big Maps, though then the ideas, and wit, were more important; the excited spontaneity was still there but at the service of those.

Paintings are terrific to be part of because they are objects, they hang on walls, they can be visited, one crowds around them, they can be possessed. None of this is true of poetry, for all its wonderfulness. There is another kind of collaboration I've done with painters, more at a distance: the painter gives me the art which suggests to me a text. Or I give him the poetry and he makes up the art. When the painter works from my text the results are often surprising and gratifying, like seeing oneself dressed as a Chinese emperor in a trick photograph; though naturally I prefer the first, in which I get to be inspired by what is presented to me, demanding I make it even more beautiful with words. Or more intellectually interesting, even, as was the case, I thought so anyway, with Alex Katz's drawings for *Interlocking Lives*. In any case, to change it and give it a new life.

I also write plays and have always liked having painters take part in those. A subject I find dramatically exciting, the history of the construction of a city, for example, I don't see how to put it onstage without artists there building it as the play goes on. This is what happened in *The Construction of Boston*. Bob Rauschenberg brought people and weather to the city, Tinguely brought architecture, Niki de St. Phalle brought art. My text was a seventeenth-eighteenth century masque- and pageant-like verse celebration of the events of the city's rise. When Tinguely had a show at the Jewish Museum (1964), I wrote a play in which his machines were among the main characters. The artists' works were right at the center of these two plays; for other plays painters did sets, sometimes remarkable extravagant sets like Red Grooms's city of Shanghai for *The Red Robins;* this set prompted me to write a new scene so Shanghai would be on stage longer.

Collaborating means you're working but not alone; or, you could say, you're with others but you get to work. When it goes well, it's very pleasant. The time in which I lived must have something to do with this work I did, and the particular friends

I had, as well. The time I started working with painters was the sixties, but when I started doing collaborative works was in the early fifties; these were with other poets, John Ashbery and Frank O'Hara. That was exhilarating. It seemed natural enough to then work with a painter but I doubt I'd have done it so soon (ever?) if Frank and Larry hadn't done their collaboration *Stones.* Their work gave me an idea of something I wanted to do with Larry. Frank did collaborations with many other painters. Among the general reasons for our excitement about collaborating (poets and painters both), two seem fairly clear: one was our admiration for the surrealists, who had done collaborations and who, poets and painters, influenced each other in all kinds of ways; and the other was our feeling so excited and so energetic and so full of ourselves and our work and at the same time our being so unrecognized and our having just about no audience but each other, so what could be better than to do works together. We couldn't think about the "market," which almost didn't exist for us, so we could rush along creating art and literature in a sort of cultural, and certainly economic and critical, vacuum.

The excited feelings didn't stop, though, when there was more recognition, and more money, at least for the painters. The painters were still "rebellious" and determinedly avant-garde, and now we had a new element to work in, the element of power (slight), of the illusion of having the means to do just about anything we wanted. Huge paintings of girls' faces by Alex Katz adorned the top stories of Times Square buildings, Tinguely displayed his self-destructing Universe Machine in the Arizona desert, Christo began hanging wrappings over monuments and mountains. It was hard for poetry to follow art to these places, but that partly illusory elixir of possibility and power had something to do with *The Construction of Boston* and *The Tinguely Machine Mystery,* and with Jim Dine's and my project of a huge book with every page a different material (steel, wood, glass, etc.).

One thing collaboration gives is the frequent if not constant feeling of being surprised, of being led where one had no idea one was going, and finding that being there one has something interesting to say. One may get this feeling writing alone, though in collaborations it's almost a given, part of the project. Obviously some artists and some writers like this kind of situation more than others. For precise planners, for artists with a clearly defined point they want to make, for the obsessed and the visionary, the kinds of collaborations I've described may not have so much appeal. If, as to me, they are appealing, even inspiring, then one is lucky to find painters, as I was very lucky to have found Larry, Alex, and others, who like them too.

An odd (artistic) sort of greed (one could be kinder and say it's hunger) might be a cause of the wish to collaborate, to expand one's territories, to make more things and of different kinds. Poetry is limited to paper (and voices) why not have it in the trees and in the clouds, in everyday conversation (was it really there in Heian Japan?), accompanying the statues and the columns of temples and palaces? But here, I suppose, one is getting close to the crazy idea of art's replacing life (the universe as museum and a theatre). Not much chance of this overthrow from modest works on paper; adding a little pleasure is probably more like it (to the participants and, hopefully, to the viewers).

For a prejudiced point of view in *favor* of collaborations, there is this of Lautréamont's, which I take the liberty of assuming may be applied to poets and painters as well as just to poets

> *La poésie doit être faite par tous. Non par un. Pauvre Hugo! Pauvre Racine!*
> *Pauvre Coppée! Pauvre Corneille! Pauvre Boileau! Pauvre Scarron! Tics, tics, et tics.*
>
> Lautéamont, *Poésies: Preface à un livre futur.*

Notes on the Collaborations

Works with Larry Rivers

The earliest collaborations seem to be lost, the ones on which Larry and I worked together on canvas or paper. After that, we worked together in various ways. Larry did covers for seven of my books, and for *When the Sun Tries to Go On* he also did nine collages—Larry, with his painting, his conversation, his presence generally, was, like a few other friends, very much a part of this 1953 poem (he appears in it as himself and as "Cary Shivers"). For *Diana* Larry did the art first, then I wrote the poem; for *In Bed* and *A Song to the Avant-Garde* the texts came first. *Cows* we did together looking at cows on a Long Island farm. *Diana* is a "jump-up" book: it folds flat, and when you lift the cover the scene of Diana at the window jumps up. Larry's Diana was a friend of his, mine is the goddess. *A Song to the Avant-Garde* is a selection of plays from the book *One Thousand Avant-Garde Plays*. Larry first thought of making a movie of *In Bed* but then decided on a painting. (Rudy Burckhardt later did make a movie of *In Bed*). Larry acted in three of my plays—he was a police chief, Lyndon Johnson, and a talking dog.

With Red Grooms

The Thing To Do was done for a book of rubber-stamp art/poetry collaborations. Red Grooms took my already-written poem and made it into a conversation between a child and a dog. This work gave us the idea for a whole series of Grooms versions of short poems by me, of which the only other two completed so far as I know are *At the Railroad Station* and *Flowers of Evil*.

Eight Maps. These are part of an ambitious project that wasn't completed. Also part of this project is a very large oil painting of the Athens Cemetery (the *Kereimikos*), with almost life-size tombs and inscriptions. There is also a styrofoam global map (*Mappemonde*), as well as an uncompleted *Children's Poetry Map of China*. Of the maps in this exhibition, three are of Ancient Greece, one of modern Greece, two of France, one of Africa, one of the State of Virginia. Eventually, I thought, we could make maps of every place and everything. There were ideas for many more maps, including a large-scale "talking" world map and an *Ice-Cream Map of Italy*. Unfortunately we had to stop at ten maps. Grooms and I worked together on these maps in his studio. After the ten maps were made, I made a book of them, a sort of Poetic Atlas, writing poetry and prose to go with various details of the maps. (Red Grooms also made sets for two of my lays, *Guinevere or the Death of the Kangaroo* and *The Red Robins.*)

With Alex Katz

Alex did the sets and costumes for my play *George Washington Crossing the Delaware.* To multiply the British and American forces onstage, he made a number of colorful and convincing flat wooden statues of men and horses. He also made one of the sets for *The Red Robins.* For *Interlocking Lives,* Alex gave me a set of twenty-one drawings. I wrote five stories each illustrated by the same twenty-one drawings, as a sort of contribution to the philosophical problem of the relation of picture to text.

With Jean Tinguely

These little works by Tinguely aren't actually collaborations but letters he sent me in the course of our doing together *The Construction of Boston* and *The Tinguely Machine Mystery.*

With Roy Lichtenstein

Homes was conceived as a book of "home-advertisement" drawings by Roy Lichtenstein accompanied by a correspondingly flat and somewhat simple-minded poetic text by me. We didn't finish this project, but Roy did this one drawing and I wrote this first sketch of a poem.

With Joe Brainard

Joe Brainard did a comic book with a number of poets; this comic book was published by "C" Press and was called *C Comics.* (Later there was a second issue, *C Comics Two*) Joe and I did six comic pages. Our comics were either nostalgic parodies or a certain kind of distortion and dislocation (like *Banjo Bar*). For *The Essay* Joe gave me a book of already-drawn comics and I filled in conversation balloons and other spaces.

With Jim Dine

For *The Blue Sky Is Bread To The Scarf,* Jim Dine showed me an early version of the print and I made up some words to go with it. The other two Dine works here are part of a project we did for *Art News.* I was asked to write an essay about Dine but decided instead on a sort of exaggerated and parodic interview with him. The two pages here are the cover and some of Jim Dine's answers to my questions. We had plans for a number of ambitious works which we never realized, among them a book of poems of which each page was a different kind of fabric, plastic, or metal (I remember the copper, steel, and leather pages) and a Dine version (for Multiples) of a somewhat Monopoly-like board game I had made up called *The End of the Evening.*

With Katherine Koch

Katherine and I worked on *Andrew Goes to Rome* in Rome, in 1978. We wanted to get a sort of illuminated-manuscript effect—with a brief, simple text and a lot of color and detail in the artwork surrounding it. The *Duplications* cover shows a duplicate city of Venice in the Peruvian Andes, one of the main locales of the mock-epic poem. The cover for *Hotel Lambosa* was made from a family photograph taken around 1957, the time of a number of stories in the book. The two studies for the cover are from another photograph from the same time.

With Fairfield Porter

R-Rose is one of the fifteen or so watercolor studies Fairfield Porter made for the cover of *Rose, Where Did You Get That Red?,* a book about teaching children to write poetry.

With Nell Blaine

Prints / Poems (1953) was my first book, part of a series of books by poets and painters John Myers published at the Tibor De Nagy Gallery. Others in the series were books by

Frank O'Hara and Larry Rivers and by John Ashbery and Jane Freilicher.

With Angelo Savelli

The Bricks was one of ten poems for which Angelo Savelli made low-relief paper sculptures for a book called *Dieci Poeti americani.*

With Al Leslie

The book *Permanently* was one of a series of four published by Richard Miller and Floriano Vecchi at Tiber Press. Other poets in the series were James Schuyler, Frank O'Hara, and John Ashbery, and the other artists, Grace Hartigan, Mike Goldberg, and Joan Mitchell. I gave Al Leslie the poems and then he made the silk-screen prints.

With Rory McEwen

Rory and I had several ideas for a collaboration. One was a book of paintings of and poems about butterflies. I read up on butterflies and wrote some short poems but later we decided instead on a book of autumn leaves. Rory sent me from London photographs of his paintings of leaves and I shuffled them around and gazed at them for quite some time until I could write a poem to go with them. Rory also did a huge cloth curtain backdrop full of flowers for the Isola Non Trovata scene of *The Red Robins.*

With Bertrand Dorny

Bertrand Dorny sent me from France five copies of the (artistically) finished book and I added a text to go with it. I chose a story, "Gilberte," from *Hotel Lambosa,* because I liked the idea of that one story's being a whole book and because its theme of Paris/New York seemed interesting with Dorny's collages.

Writing for the Stage:

An Interview with Allen Ginsberg

Ginsberg: *What will the text of this play look like in a hundred years?*

Koch: I don't know anything about the future. Why do you ask me that?

Reading through eyes a hundred years hence, won't the nonsense, the contradictory humor, seem incomprehensible?

First, I intend the play not for people a hundred years from now but for people now living. Secondly—you seem to be tricking me into talking about the future whether I want to or not—it seems more likely that the logic and rationality of today will seem incomprehensible to people of the future rather than the dissociations, that is, if one can judge by the way art and poetry and music have been moving in the past hundred years. Twenty years ago, when I started teaching, none of my students could understand John Ashbery's poetry. Many now find the same poems easy to read. The nonrational associations that Rimbaud wrote down, a hundred years ago seem to me in certain ways now more comprehensible, sensible, and useful than the philosophic and scientific treatises of his time.

From *The New York Times* (Jan. 8, 1978) as Kenneth Koch's play *The Red Robins* began a three-week run at St. Clement's Theatre in New York.

What's the deep plot of The Red Robins?

I'd rather tell you the superficial plot.

Why?

That's what the plot is. There is no hidden meaning. Frank O'Hara said something about David Smith's work that seems relevant to what I intend my play to be like. In Smith's steel sculpture, O'Hara said "unification is approached by inviting the eye to travel over the complicated surface exhaustively, rather than inviting it to settle on the whole first and then explore certain details."

Can you give me an example of complication of surface?

A couple of examples. In scene 3 of act 1 there's a tiger hunt. The tiger escapes from the Red Robins . . .

Before we go on, I guess you should explain who or what the Red Robins are.

They are a group of young Americans—Jim, Bob, Lyn, Jill, and others—who have gone to Asia in search of adventure, truth, and happiness. They're in no specific time, and are unconnected to specific political events. They're without developmental problems, they're full of passion, excitement, and yearning. They are pilots and each has his or her own airplane. They are in some ways like the heroes and heroines of boys' and girls' adventure books. My novel *The Red Robins*, from which the play is very freely adapted, was partly inspired by such adventure books.

How long did you work on the novel? Why are you so devoted to your imagination of the Red Robins? Is that why you put them into a play?

One reason I put them into a play is that I liked the novel so much. I worked on the novel for about fifteen years. And in the time I was writing it the characters and everything about them became very rich for me and suggestive. When I began the play there was a whole world of places, persons, and feelings I could use. It was like a country I knew. I found that inspiring.

How does the play change your fancy of the Red Robins?

Well, the play is simpler, airier, and more direct. It also has a different kind of music—it's mostly written in a kind of heroic Shakespearean blank verse. The relative simplicity and the music make it more what I like my plays to be.

What do you mean by your answer?

In the novel, the Red Robins are part of a very complicated chronicle which lasts a long time and is written in a variety of styles. In the play, I take their main characteristics and their main passions and have them express those in a high poetic way. I like plays to be epic, high spirited, even a little operatic. One of the best plays I ever saw was a British production of Marlowe's *Tamburlaine*. The conquest of Asia taking place on stage, in action and in that marvelous poetry, was very moving.

Let's go back to complication of surface in your play.

As I was saying, in act 1, scene 3, during the tiger hunt the tiger escapes from the Red Robins who have almost caught him. Then the tiger reappears onstage alone and delivers a soliloquy which begins "My name is Mike, and I am a man-eating tiger." After Mike speaks, there are speeches by a Tropical Plant, a Gland, a Stone, and an Undiscovered Possibility named Elia.

The next scene is in a Malay hospital room where Lyn, a beautiful young girl pilot, is recovering from a nightmare brought on by a fever: her nightmare was the previous scene. This is not clear until Lyn says so. Mike the Tiger, however, continues to appear in the play as a real tiger.

Another example of complicated surface: in the same hospital scene after Lyn has gone to sleep, Jim who loves Lyn and is a poet, sits down and writes a love scene between Jill, another girl Red Robin and Santa Claus, a middle-aged former international criminal who has joined the Red Robins while they are adventuring through Asia. This love scene is acted out onstage, while Jim writes it, by Jill and Santa Claus—who, of course, are real characters in the play. It is not clear, nor meant to be, whether the whole play which the audience is seeing is written by Jim or not, or whether it may all be a dream of Lyn. This complication does not, I believe, make something simple less clear, but is an approach to making clear something which is not simple.

What is that something which is not simple—can you make that explicit?

Probably not without being somewhat unclear. However, I will try. There are many things in life and in literature, as everybody knows, which indicate that things are not always what they seem, and that the truest and fullest perception of reality is not available to our reason alone, or even to our completely awakened consciousness. Many people find this situation a source of anxiety and sorrow, but it can be seen also as a source of great pleasure, and of a great chance for creation and truly constructive artistic activity. There are some important parts of what I consider to be the truth which I think can best come from or can only be communicated by works of art. The reason that my communication of these things is sometimes comic and perhaps seemingly inappropriately happy and high-spirited is that writing, insofar as it is the discovery and conquest of these things, makes me excited and happy. The comic element may also come partly from my not wishing to give up any of the Heroic, Romantic enthusiasm which seems the most appropriate way of expressing the strongest things I feel—and at the same time being obliged to avoid the conventional situations, languages, and form in which these feelings have already been expressed. Popeye is a better hero, for my purposes, than Hercules.

So that's why you have as heroic characters and villains the Easter Bunny and Santa Claus—the same esthetic?

Yes, they are both imaginary beings in whose reality I believed during important years of my life—from about two to six. As such, even their slightest characteristics, such as the Rabbit's ears, Santa Claus's sleigh, are full of strong meaning for me. In a way that the characteristics of, say Zeus and Helen of Troy, or say Johnny Appleseed are not.

What about Jehovah and Christ?

Probably because of the way they were presented to me, they had less chance to become imaginatively real to me.

In your play is a character named Elia, whom you referred to earlier as an Undiscovered Possibility. Elia says, "I don't even know whether I'm a solid, a liquid, a gas, an idea, or an emotion. I am motionless . . . I know nothing about myself. Please find me. I will love you if you do—if I am capable of that." Is that you, basically? That seemed a particularly endearing familiar self.

Well, I did write those words and I know what it's like to feel that way. But that is Elia's only speech in the play, and Elia is part of a dream—it's certainly not the main way I feel.

What's the main influence on your Heroic Romantic euphony?

Shakespeare and Marlowe.

So under the surface of your comic rhetoric flows the stream of Renaissance eloquence.

I hope so. I even hope that the two are indistinguishable. The Renaissance English dramatic-poet line seems the ideal medium, instrument, for expressing strong feelings—the comic element that becomes part of it for me is what I need to let me express myself.

This has been your oratorical tactic all along from Thank You *on. How do you reconcile it with the antiromantic stylistics of William Carlos Williams which has influenced us all?*

I love Williams's work, but I don't think, obviously, that it or anyone else's work exhausts the possibilities of poetry, nor does it cover or deal with a great many things in my experience.

For instance?

For instance, all the experience in the play we're talking about. I think I like to enter a poem at the point when Williams is about to leave it, to stay with the romantic exhilaration and see what happens when it doesn't end. One thing that led me to this is Williams's poetry, with its emphasis on happiness.

Santa Claus, in your play, in a scene in Shanghai, says ". . . There in the North / Is where the Slimy Green Things Are." How come a guy your age is writing plays about "We must find the Slimies."

It's not necessarily a man my age who wrote that. Paul Valéry says that a poem is written by someone not the poet to someone who is not the reader. Furthermore, confess, Allen, that you might be afraid if you were awakened in the middle of the night by someone saying "The slimy green things are here!"

I confess I never thought of that. In your play, one character, a Man in a Yellow Coat, says, "What can it mean, that we are born into paradise or Nothingness . . . ?" Isn't that like Buddhist wisdom?

Yes, but I think, rather than being Buddhist wisdom, it refers to that kind of wisdom. It's one of the many references to different kinds of views of life in the play. It goes back to something like Frank O'Hara's remark about David Smith. I think you have a tendency to look for a meaning beneath the surface of my work, whereas the meaning is really that surface. A wise Buddhist remark instantly followed by the appearance of a girl pilot talking about a summer resort, has a different meaning from a wise Buddhist remark followed by another one.

The surface playfulness that struck me sharpest was the moment in the scene when Lyn, the girl pilot, suddenly appears in the Shanghai Garden of the Man in the Yellow Coat and he says to her "What? Who are you? What?" and she says to him out of her summer-resort day-dream, "The railroad train stopped. It looked like a smokestack. Then green spots started to appear all over its wheels and sides." Then he says, out of nowhere, "Lyn, you must find the ring!" and she wakes up, saying "What ring?" Could you explain what's happening?

Yes. It's very clear when you see it on stage. Lyn, looking for the Slimy Green Things, accidentally comes on a beautiful city garden in which a man in a yellow coat—he's a retired diplomat—is meditating aloud. This puts her in a dreamy mood and a strange memory comes back to her. Her reverie is interrupted by the man's recognizing her as one of the world-renowned Red Robins and his wishing to help her by giving her information about the Ring of Destiny, which the Robins will need in order to reach Tin Fan, the City of Perfect Happiness, located somewhere in the middle of China.

The adventure book genre this story idea comes from, you're not putting it down, are you? You're treating your early imagination sympathetically?

There's an intensity and a purity about such books that I take seriously.

There's been something of that in all the stages of your poetry. In Thank You, *for example, I think that's one of your happy poetic periods. And influential. It was a light expansion that encouraged a whole lot of people to follow their own fancy in composition, to talk about their own feelings and sensations without being bothered too much by preconceived ideas of literature, symbolic poems filled with academic despair. Your poem "Fresh Air" came out about the same time as "Howl." I thought that we'd hit on the same explosion of fearless humor, poetic energy, expansive and unchecked, as the Good Grey Poet might say . . . In your poetry and plays there are very free associations. Is your intention to activate a similar set of associations in the reader's head, or to present him with a surface artifact (maybe with a hint of resonance mysteriously humming somewhere between poet and reader)?*

I don't know. I suppose I trust my associations the way I imagine a composer of music must trust his.

Trust your associations to arrive at exquisite language, or trust your associations to be similar to reader's? I'm asking a question that I use in composition.

I trust my associations to make something that's beautiful. It's been my experience that when one does that other people can often get something from it.

Your teaching of poetry writing to children and to old people—is it an extrapolation from this way of composition?

Yes.

This trust in association is a recognizable element in classic poetry: Shakespeare, etc.—Is there some twentieth-century difference wherein this element takes off on its own and becomes dominant in poetic art? It does seem to be universal Method, since Einstein, Joyce, O'Hara, or even Rimbaud's association of vowel-colors which you paraphrase in The Red Robins.

I think the change is that the associations, instead of being used to enrich or explore an already decided-on subject tend to become the subject—or, if not that, then a way of finding the subject.

That's a fantastic leap from previous centuries—or is there a precedent?

It's one reason I've always thought that this was a great time in which to write poetry. Of course I haven't lived in any other time.

You've always lived in a world of friendly artists. Now, in The Red Robins, *collaboration with painters is part of the drama—who's creating pictures for your stage?*

Red Grooms has done sets for the City of Shanghai, the Jungle, a Remote Pacific Island, and an airport on a plateau somewhere in Asia. Roy Lichenstein made a large silver-and-blue airplane, Jane Freilicher made the Shanghai City Garden, Rory McEwen made and sent from London the set for the Isola Non Trovata, an island the Red Robins visit which is filled with vowel-flowers. Alex Katz designed a five-foot high wall of robins with an electric blue sky behind them. Katherine Koch, my daughter twenty-two years old, who also did the cover for my book *The Duplications,* made the Washington set—the Capitol, with flowering cherry trees. And Vanessa James made the sky, the mountains of Asia, the great Asian resort hotel (the Coluhdson), the ocean liner, and the ocean. She also coordinated the work of all the other artists. The reason it seemed appropriate to have so many artists working on one play, aside from the general excitement of such a venture, is that sets that were works of art created by different people might reinforce the variety of dramatic changes of place and of feeling in the play.

Have you last thoughts about the play I haven't unearthed?

Yes. Probably—but two obvious ones. First, it owes a lot to the director and to the actors. Don Sanders's direction is so good it inspired me to write several new scenes.

How's Taylor Mead doing? He's my favorite comedian after Chaplin.

Taylor's a wonderful actor. He plays five or six parts in the play, including Mike the Tiger, the Slimy Green Things, Jill's father, and Ni Shu the Chinese Philosopher.

What's your second unspoken thought?

It's a question. Allen I want you to be in the play—the part of the dog in act 2, scene 2. Will you do it?

Arf. Arf.

V

An Interview with Jordan Davis

I interviewed Kenneth Koch in the summer of 1995. What follows here are some of his remarks on the various subjects I asked him about. These included questions about his life, his education, his taste, his influences, particular poems, his writing of plays and stories and long poems, his use of rhymes, the frequency of love poems in his work, his narrative poems, his conception of humor and the comic. I present them here more or less by subject (not strictly) and in no particular order.—
Jordan Davis

When I read Louis Untermeyer's anthology *Modern American and British Poetry* I liked almost all the poets in it. They had skill I'd never dreamed of. I was very young (seventeen). I was like somebody from a country where there are no machines coming to a place where he sees cars and power saws and telephones. I was astonished at what these poets could do.

Literary Criticism

Without Pound I don't know if I'd ever have read Provençal poetry or ever have read Chinese poetry and Japanese Noh plays so seriously. As it was, he made them part of the great secret literary fiesta of my time. I spent lots of (happy if somewhat uncomprehending) afternoons and nights at the old Chinese theatre under the Manhattan Bridge. I translated troubador poems to be sung. I fastened myself to Golding's Ovid—(Pound said it was the most beautiful book in English). Nobody else was telling me anything, it seemed. Pound's writing had a way of moving right into my head and bossing me around. I went anywhere I could to see a Noh play put on. Helpful in another way was George Saintsbury's *History of English Prosody* (recommended by Pound). Saintsbury for me changed the deadly dry technical part of poetry into a lively joyful even sexy part. Variations in lines of unrhymed iambic pentameter became as exciting as the variations in the *Art of the Fugue,* Debussy's snowdrifts, dissonances, sprechstimme, Chopin's legato or lack of it. Meter, which had seemed a task—and a task, probably, to be "modern" to be avoided, was, it became clear, a big party, a lot of costumes to try on.

Influences

Among the poets who gave me early ideas of what poetry was were Shelley and Yeats. A bit later came Eliot. I remember being spellbound when I first read *The Waste Land.* It seemed more than a mere work. With its vagueness, its clarity, and its dissociations, it was like a big spacious mystery voyage (I didn't care, almost didn't notice what it said). I'd forgotten about that. I've gotten used to being a little annoyed by Eliot and forgot how marvelous *The Waste Land* is—or was. Shantih Shantih Shantih. It seemed to go beyond human possibilities. Eliot later was useful to "write against." In an Eliot-dominated poetic ambience, even the slightest sensations of happiness or pleasure seemed rare and revolutionary poetic occasions. If happy, positive, excited poetry were the "scene," I might have been looking for the nuances of the losses and sorrows in my life for the subjects of poems.

After I read Whitman I felt I could write about anything— I love Whitman's tone

I am the poet of the body and I am the poet of the soul

I see the great secretaries

Houses and rooms are full of perfumes

I can't imagine this man, hardly at all. His lines seem to rise from the pages of a book like trumpet sounds from microscopic chips embedded there. No it's really a person, a slightly strident or corny one, but where did he get that tone? It sounds a little manic, euphoric, but full of so much odd and interesting thought. It's as if some wild Marlovian hero had wandered into nineteenth-century America.

French Poetry

Discovering French poetry was like discovering a new kind of art. When I was much younger I thought about the excitement of finding a new art altogether. French poetry was a little bit like this. There were fiction, nonfiction, drama, poetry, and French poetry. An odd thing was that its classic phases were as wonderful to me as its avant-garde ones. From Racine: "Pour qui sont ces serpents qui sifflent sur vos têtes?" (For whom are those snakes intended that are whistling on top of your heads?) I was fascinated by the alexandrine. For one thing, you get to go on for longer than with a pentameter. Then too there was the restraint and the elegance in highly charged situations (those snakes) unlike anything I'd known in life or in poetry in English. I loved du Bellay, pleased and complaining about Rome. Lamartine was able, say in "Le Lac," to detach a *sentiment,* a strong feeling, and then reconstruct it as a large beautiful aquarelle or pavane. I heard spooky voices coming out of these French poems. Who were these people (Lamartine—*on ramait en silence*), who were so young and so grand? Were they some form of me? They had to be connected to me in some way—but to whom could *I* ever say such things? I loved a few medieval works, especially "Aucassin et Nicolette"—I liked the story and the poetry (it alternated between poetry and prose). I even liked the spelling—

Qui vauroit bons vers oir
del deport du viel antif
de deus biax enfans petis
Nicholete et Aucassins
des grans paines qu'il soufri . . .

My fascination with the spelling may be related to the fact
that my French at the time (my first year in France, when I
was twenty-five) was in some way "medieval" too, the way
being my uncertainties about which word was which and
about spelling and pronouncing them. The New French po-
etry that overwhelmed me was first Apollinaire, whose po-
ems I sat for days figuring out in Cincinnati, Ohio (my home
town), before I went to Paris for the first time. Once I was
there, there were wonderful French paperbacked books, al-
most as cheap as a glass of wine, and I remember reading
them the way I drank those glasses, too, not too much but
quite naturally day after day. Max Jacob's "Cornet à dés" was
funny and gorgeous—

Et toi, Dostoievsky!

Mysterious shadowy Reverdy had a poetry that almost wasn't
there. Éluard was a wonderful possession, with his seriousness
about the eroticism of everything. Breton had lines

Si seulement il faisait du soleil cette nuit

that I liked as well as anything. I loved Perse, though he was
distant, flinging out phrases like the unending surf. I liked
Char but didn't understand him and still don't. He is an
encouragement, though, for the dry southern climate of his
language and for its unyielding, even stony kind of insistence
on saying something not clear. (I liked Ponge and I liked
Michaux.) Thinking of them now, I begin to have some idea
of how odd these poets were, where their art was coming
from, what the personalities that went into making their po-
etry must have been like. At that time, though, in summer,
autumn, and winter sunny and rainy days of Paris and Aix

en Provence in 1950 and 1951 they affected me the way girls affect boys (and vice versa). I was just crazy about them, about their attractiveness, their secrets, their spontaneous generosities and enthusiasms, their taking, as it were, one off into the corner quite unexpectedly for a kiss. My crush on them extended to some extent to the French language and almost everything written in it, even Virgil's *Eclogues,* translated into French which I read in Aix.

Italian Poetry

My favorite twentieth-century Italian poet is Guido Gozzanno, who lived just at the beginning of the century. He seems a poet who by being so good shows how strange and unpredictable poetryland is. Gozzanno is mild, "psychological," ironic, "romantic," things that in combination one might expect to do him in, but there he is, a great one. Montale liked him a lot. But my Italian isn't good enough for my taste to be taken seriously. I did read a great deal of Ariosto and was much affected by him. I like a number of Renaissance poets of course, too—Cavalcanti (more medieval I suppose), Poliziano—"Chi non sa come e fatto il paradiso / Guardi l'Ipollita mia negli occhi fiso"; Petrarch (pastorella). Just as I fell in love with French poetry in 1950, I fell in love with Italian Renaissance poetry in 1954, when Janice and I spent six months in Italy. I remember coming home with a little gray book I'd just bought (edizioni einaudi) with the title *Tutta la Poesia Italiana.* Janice and I were both really excited at having this treasure in our hands. Within a few moments though we saw that Poliziano was not the editor but the author and these were all the poems HE had written in Italian, not all the poems everyone had. But that was good enough.

Poetic Form

It's true that sometimes I write in standard poetic forms and sometimes I don't. I like doing both. The worst is not feeling any music coming with the words one is writing, enough music to make it convincing. There were a year or two when I couldn't feel any of this music. That was awful. The music has to be there. I can look for sense afterward, or along the way. But the pull of a phrase or a line is the only true sign that something worthwhile may be beginning. Whether it's in quatrains, couplets, blank verse, ottava rima, or free verse doesn't matter at all in that respect. It's like the difference between being attracted to someone at court or in a bowling alley. Along the way one may say something memorable. That is not the object of writing a poem but it's very nice

> if we make a desert
> of ourselves, we make a desert
>
> (Williams)

Humanity goes around with this in its head, one of the many delightful products of being attentive and inattentive, loose and tense at the same time as my tennis teacher used to confusingly tell me to be. When I'm revising, the outlines of what's possible are much stricter and more evident—I'm only "inspired" so far then I bump into the side of the pool. Free verse, one doesn't really write free verse nowadays any more than one practices free love. Anyway, unrhymed unmetrical verse is wonderful for getting feelings and sensations just as they occur and getting into them with your regular voice. Rhyme and meter give orchestral and otherwise festive accompaniment. Rhyme in stanzas I like for narrative poems of more than a few pages. The first poem I remember writing was a rhymed quatrain. Then when I was nine my chief work was a rhymed poem about a comic criminal named Randy Moore—

> Randy Moore was a dirty crook
> Everything valuable Randy took

(I guess he is something like my later heroes Dog Boss, Papend, and Bertha, for example.) Reading (much later) Byron and Ariosto helped me refine my rhymes beyond these. When I was about twenty I discovered (in Saintsbury really) blank verse and wrote an intensely serious poem (of about 5 pages) in it, of which I've lost track. It begins

> Peter you bastard, you know stammering
> Has implications as profound as love—

How happy I was to make *stammering* last for three syllables, two of them stressed; and the mysteriously lifted-up *you bastard* and the equally mysteriously poeticized *implications*. Soon I gave such pleasures up—the verse seemed grandiose—

I read Auden a little late. At first I found his intellectuality and also his masterful use of all kinds of forms not to my taste. Then one day I caught on to his poetry and found it irresistible. It gave the sheer pleasure of form on its own—ballads, sestinas, canzones, even *Chanson de Roland* stanzas, consonant-rhyme couplets, all those fascinating things. In a little apartment on West Tenth Street (in N.Y.) in 1948 I remember dedicating weeks to a canzone, a form which I had seen only in Auden, though Dante had written one, his poem beginning

> Amor, tu vedi ben che questa donna
> La tua virtù non cura in alcum tempo,
> Che suol dell' altre belle farsi donna . . .

It has twelve-line stanzas with only five end words in each stanza, a sort of compounded sestina. My canzone was about Persephone, her picking flowers, her kidnapping by Dis, etc. I was happy with the repetitions, at the ends of lines, of my key words: *Flowers, Hell,* I forget the rest. Auden's *Selected Poems* was for me a great poetic amusement park, a park of poetic forms to try out.

Narrative

I guess I learned how to tell three or four stories at the same time from reading *The Faerie Queene* and *Orlando Furioso,* and how to digress from reading Byron. Though Byron was the original inspiration for my writing *Ko* I didn't read him while I was writing it. I was afraid of being overwhelmed by his sophistication. He seemed to know everything about everything, and I so obviously didn't. Especially everything social and he was able to be witty about everything and I was socially unsophisticated. Frank (O'Hara) maybe could have written such a poem in Byron's way, but I don't think Frank was interested in writing a long poem in ottava rima though there's a pretty Byronesque wit and breadth and sophistication in *Biotherm*. Instead, I read Ariosto and hardly made any comments at all; I made my poem entirely plot.

Reading *Don Juan* was a startling experience. I've never liked a poem more. It's so witty and so sweet. It's so generous in the details it gives. The plot is mainly an excuse for talking, as life seems sometimes to be.

I read *Paradise Lost* late (I was twenty-five) and when I did I stayed up all night and read it all the way through. It was a very large edition with illustrations by Gustave Doré, demons and angels with great cross-hatched wings. The poem seemed stunningly big. I wrote Miltonics for weeks after I read it.

I like narratives in prose, too, of course, though the pleasures of verse are hard to make up for. But I've never felt anything lacking when I've read Stendhal. He makes prose seem like the real party the way Socrates made conversation seem like the real philosophy.

I remember John Ashbery and I were reading *The Faerie Queene* at the same time (1949 or 1950). When I asked him how he was liking it, he said it was wonderful, like reading an endless comic strip.

Comics influenced my writing. I read them as sheep graze grass. When I was ten years old my ambition was to draw comic strips. I was deterred, though, by my fear that I wouldn't be able to draw the characters so they would look the same every time. But everything about them was intriguing.

In a comic strip you can emphasize *any* detail or moment of a story—the pattern of the hero's necktie, a bus passing outside the window, a grin, a tear drop. I enjoyed doing things like that a lot in *Ko.*

Actually a few years ago I spent some months (quite a few) making some comics of my own, which I called *The Art of the Possible, Comics Mainly Without Pictures.* I was attracted to doing something like that not only because I liked comics but because the comics format suggested new ways of talking about things and dividing them up. Easiest is to show some examples—

In "Appliqué Comics," (Fig. 1) in the two top rows the words tell the story and then in the bottom rows the words are just there to designate objects. "Bosom Comics" (Fig. 2) was somewhat Calligramme-like.

"The Dead White Man" was a story in four "shots"—(figs. 3–6)

Plays

I like plays that are to be astounding in some way—that make convincing what is unusual and even, seemingly, impossible. It's hard to write and produce such works when there is no active tradition of having such works. One has to make it all up each time. Which isn't bad, is in fact exciting, but it means you have to have money, devoted actors and other helpers, a place to put them on, and then, even when you have if you have, all this, you have to find an audience, people who will look at what you've done, and who will get it, participate in it, like and dislike it, be open to it and clear and willing to see more. Still, theater in its best moments, is one of the best things. I think it is even more happiness making to write and put on a play than to see it. When you see it it ends. When you do it, it's always rehearsal. I never have been able to resist getting involved in it. I started writing "plays" when I was eleven, they were satires of our extended family life, all fairly

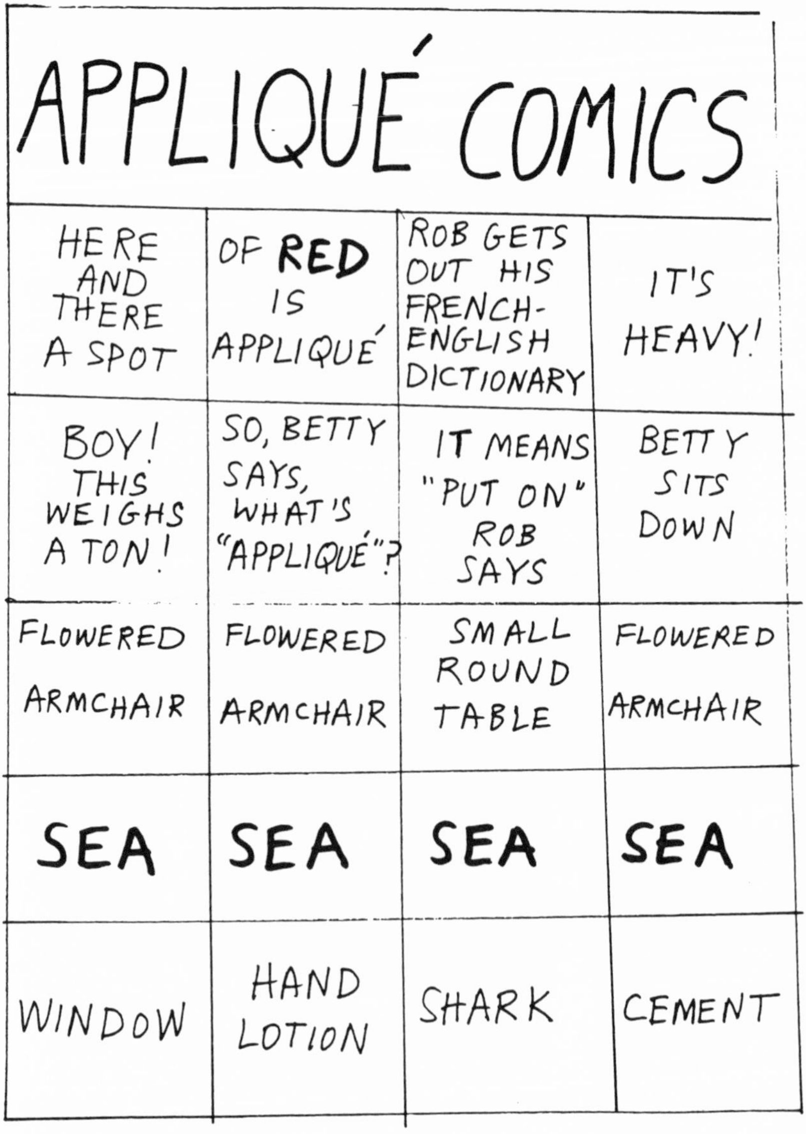

APPLIQUÉ COMICS

HERE AND THERE A SPOT	OF **RED** IS APPLIQUÉ	ROB GETS OUT HIS FRENCH-ENGLISH DICTIONARY	IT'S HEAVY!
BOY! THIS WEIGHS A TON!	SO, BETTY SAYS, WHAT'S "APPLIQUÉ"?	IT MEANS "PUT ON" ROB SAYS	BETTY SITS DOWN
FLOWERED ARMCHAIR	FLOWERED ARMCHAIR	SMALL ROUND TABLE	FLOWERED ARMCHAIR
SEA	SEA	SEA	SEA
WINDOW	HAND LOTION	SHARK	CEMENT

Fig. 1

Fig. 2

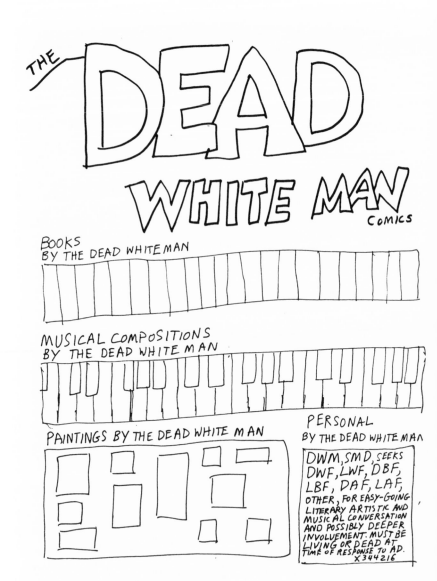

Fig. 3

Fig. 4

Fig. 5

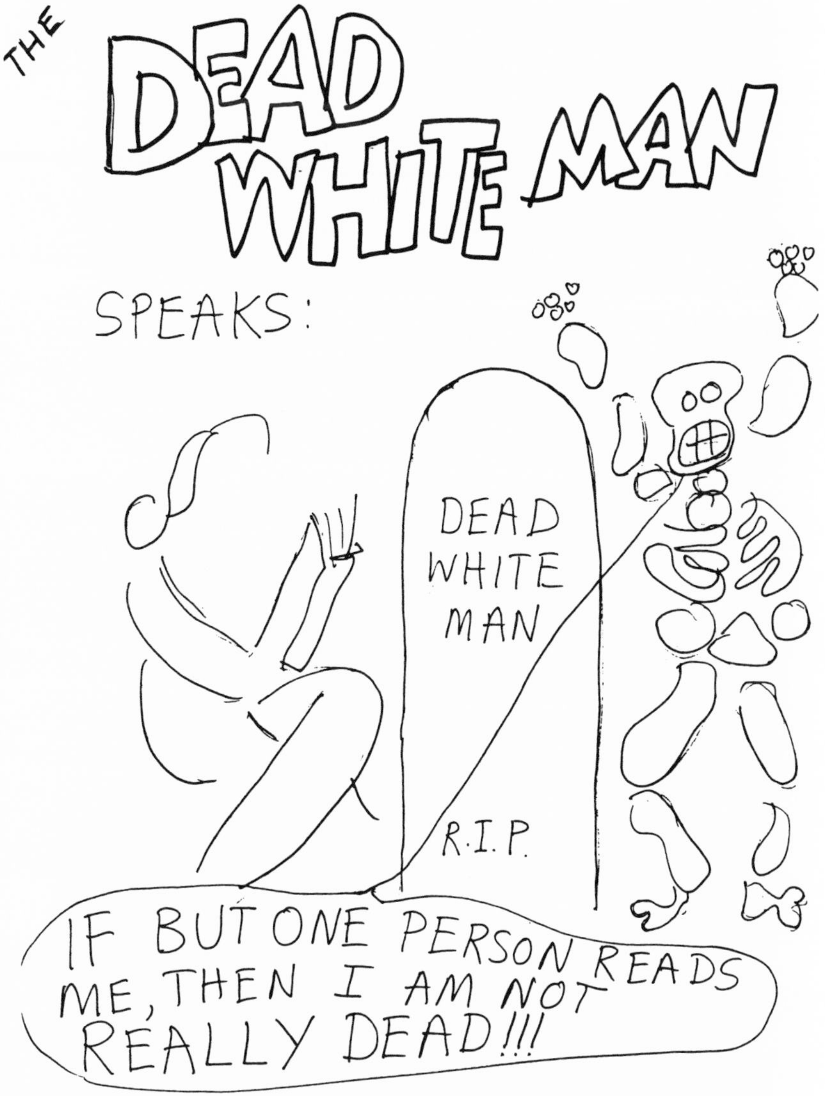
THE DEAD WHITE MAN SPEAKS:
DEAD WHITE MAN R.I.P.
IF BUT ONE PERSON READS ME, THEN I AM NOT REALLY DEAD!!!

Fig. 6

benign caricatural stuff—Uncle Nate was "nervous," Uncle Leo ate too much, etc. No one varied from his character in these early dramatic works and nothing ever happened. It was fun, I remember, writing ENTER and EXIT and ENTER AUNT MARIAN IN A RED COAT. Which reminds me of Virgil (Thomson's) wonderful discrimination—opera's all about saying good-bye and ballet is all about saying hello. From these hellos and good-byes I moved on to Yeatsean symbolic drama, in a play I wrote at Harvard, called *Little Red Riding Hood,* it was full of gongs, slow-downs, freezing in position, iambic pentameter—

> Yes, I seem to recognize the place
> As though its weather were indelible
> And formal in my mind.

As though its weather were indelible! I have to laugh at my somewhat inflated baby-poet self but how I loved those lines. I said them over and over to myself. At Harvard I was reading every verse drama I could find—Lorca, Eliot (especially *Sweeny Agonistes,* I didn't like the later ones), Yeats, Auden, Delmore Schwartz, even William Vaughan Moody . . . I was searching for the secret (one of a number of times I did that), the secret way to write a play "in poetry"; it seemed like a delicious mystery, that Shakespeare could do it, so perfectly, and that there was no way to do it now. Of course I was also reading Shakespeare, Marlowe, Webster, and the Romantic verse plays, Beddoes, Byron, Keats, Shelley. These verse dramas, though, couldn't give me what I needed to write the kind of play I wanted to write, though they showed me how to versify dramatic speech. When I finally wrote some plays I liked (*Pericles* was the first one), it was because "dramatic" and even more so "crazy" were added to or substituted for "poetic"—I read *Ubu roi* and everything was turned upside down. There is an entire scene in *Ubu* that consists of Ubu's coming onstage, saying I am going to kill everybody! then going off. It made me happy. Aunt Marian in her red coat could return! Though now, free from restrictions of family legend, she could be not simply an obsessive golfer but Aphrodite, Astarte, the Spirit of Progress and Industry, Juliet, or Herself who could be all these. Then I was also struck by Pound's and Fenellosa's translations of Noh plays and the Chinese plays I went to see downtown and, a little later, Futurist plays, in which the entire action might be turning on blinding light after a long prelude of darkness (v. *Light!* by Cangiullo). Anything that got me away from the dreary Broadway-type plays I'd been taken to see in Cincinnati and was still menaced by in the pages of the Sunday *Times*, artificial and stilted arrangements of stale persons and staler ideas; people who carped at one another, discussed issues, were false, were true. Who would ever want to write plays? of course now they have been replaced by TV shows just as horrible (I think no worse) and who would want to write plays now either? And a big problem in the theater is that if there aren't good plays to see, almost no one is ever going to be inspired to write one. In the thirty or so years I've taught writing at Columbia, I had as students quite a few good even brilliant poets and fiction writers but only one who wanted to write plays. Hard to want to if you don't see them, it's like wanting to build a temple to Isis in Idaho. "This one will be really good!" Anyway I didn't have this problem. I knew I wanted to write epic and poetic and avant-garde plays. Frank shared this interest and so to some extent did John. I wrote *George Washington Crossing the Delaware* on commission (no fee) from Larry Rivers for his son's high school production; but the auditorium collapsed, there was no place to rehearse, so the play wasn't done by high school students but by adult actors some years later. By the time I wrote the mock-heroic pentameter of *George Washington* and *Bertha* I'd been able to take in the pentameter of Marlowe's *Tamburlaine* and that of its parodists, especially Henry Carey, who wrote *Chrononhotontologos*. I didn't write much for the theater for quite a while after that, but then I saw a few of Robert Wilson's early productions (*A Letter to Queen Victoria* and *Einstein on the Beach*) and the incomprehensible mystery and grandeur of theatre got to me again and I started writing plays again. Not that I could do what Wilson did, but his example was in the air of what I did, like great fall weather. Then I wrote *The Red Robins* (a dramatic version of my novel) and Don Sanders directed it. For him I wrote *The New Diana,* another "full-length" play. When I wrote *One Thousand Avant-Garde Plays* (there are actually only 112 of them), I had the idea, of course it is only in the plays and I can't explain it, that *everything,* almost absolutely everything was potentially dramatic and could be made into a play. This insight came to me from watching actors, and moments, in my plays while they were being rehearsed—by Don Sanders and, later, by Barbara Vann—from my being illuminated and excited simply by the way an actress peeked out from behind a door or the way an actor (in this case it was Taylor Mead in *The Red Robins*) said hello. Also I noticed I could be in tears from watching a TV movie for thirty seconds and laughing happily after switching to a different one for the same amount of time. Why not get this on stage, in a way that wasn't accidental? The practical problem was finding people willing to get dressed up go out take a cab and spend $100 to spend three minutes in a theatre, because that's about how long each play lasted. This is an example of why poetry poses fewer problems to the artistic experimenter. When the plays were done Barbara Vann did seventy-two of them in one evening. Other productions have included ten or five. The play I wrote this year, *Edward and Christine*—ah, all I can say about it is that I can't wait to see it produced, which it is far from being, no theater, no money, no nothing as yet. It seems to me there are some great directors around but I don't have the same impression about new plays. The great directors often do old works or adaptations or conglomerates of old works or else use texts less interesting than the skills they deploy in staging them. Brilliant, life-enhancing moments there certainly are in these gorgeous performances. Peter Brook's *Mahabharata* may be the best play I've ever seen; Ariane Mnouchkine's Shakespeares are astonishing; Luca Ronconi won eternal glory for me with his *Orlando Furioso* in which people being rushed back and forth standing on flat trucks shout out lines of Ariosto's epic. I've already spoken of Robert Wilson.

The first play I saw that knocked me out was a Royal Shakespeare Company production of *Tamburlaine I & II* in New

York. Having all of Asia (and more, in Tamburlaine's vaulting ambition!) on stage instead of a disgruntled couple was suggestive of a lot.

I think the one person who has given me more pleasure in the theater than anybody else is George Balanchine. My friends and I used to go to Balanchine's ballets very often in the 1960s. Sometimes we'd sneak in (without paying) at the end of intermission. I remember the absolute joy I felt once coming in out of "nowhere" (that's what it seemed like) and seeing two of Balanchine's dancers high in the air. The floor of the stage didn't seem to exist for Balanchine, just the space above it. His work kept stressing this impossibly beautiful world which in fact, being as it was and enduring so, became, or was all along, completely possible, in any case a part of the possible. I remember Larry Rivers's being angry at Balanchine, and at Edwin Denby along with him, for being so stuck on this "ideal" world—"It's not everything!" said Larry but that is a part of his story and not of this one.

I love opera but there is nobody I've ever seen do opera the way Balanchine did ballet. That's too bad. Maybe it's not possible. I liked what Peter Brook did with *Carmen*. Anyway opera at its best gave me ideas of what a play could be like.

So did churches. I was in Mexico when I realized that a church was a theater, the altar the stage, etc. Not a new insight but it got me to have interesting ideas and feelings while looking at a *lot* of Mexican churches.

So did certain plays I read but didn't see on stage—Strindberg's "crazy" plays (*Spook Sonata, the Dream Play*); all the Medieval English Mystery and Morality Plays; Hardy's *The Dynasts*, with its huge scope and stage directions (The French army descend the slopes of the Pyrenees and enter under a stormy sky); Pirandello; and of course Chekhov.

Teaching

What relation there is between my teaching and my poetry? I never tried to teach anything in a poem before the poems in *The Art of Love,* the instructional tone of those poems came to me from the lectures I was giving and the books I was using at that time on how to teach children to write poetry. As I wrote out sentences, those instructional sentences began to have funny interesting tones and angles, began to have a physical existence that could make them pleasant to use in poetry—

> All this suggests the possibility of teaching literature in the schools in conjunction with writing. (*Wishes, Lies, and Dreams*)

> Nailing a woman to the wall causes too much damage
> (Not to the wall but to the woman)
>
> ("The Art of Love")

The instructional dry sound tends to make anything seem plausible—

> You may wish to fire ten cannons at once

It was another way to bring everything I wanted to into a poem.

Teaching itself didn't seem interesting to me until I'd been doing it for a few years. Before that it seemed dry, even slightly dead. Instead, I imagined such careers as being a stand-up comedian (I never even tried this one out); owning and operating a motel that would be open only three or four months a year and I'd have the rest of the time off to write (someone told me I'd have to keep the rooms clean, which I hadn't thought of, and I gave up the idea); writing commercial fiction, my first idea in this regard being what used to be known as "pulp" fiction after the kind of paper used in the magazines in which such fiction was printed—True Detective, Spicy Western, Weird Tales, etc. However I tried to write pulp fiction and could write only parodies of it. It was lucky that once I started to teach I got to like it enough to make myself good at it.

The books I wrote about teaching I found very hard to write. The introduction to *Wishes, Lies, and Dreams* (which is about thirty pages) took more than six months, and the introduction to *Rose, Where Did You Get That Red?* took almost as long. I had always had the idea before *Wishes, Lies, and Dreams* that I was unable to write clear prose. But I forced myself to do it. I had to be clear if I wanted my experiences to do any good.

Styles

It's true that I've written poetry in a number of different styles. Joyce's writing in so many styles in *Ulysses* was exciting to me and all sorts of parodies. The revolutionary ideas in linguistics and cultural anthropology seemed right, too, I mean the ones I encountered when I was in college and shortly after, ideas that the style, even the language a work was written in to a significant extent determined its content. I was attracted to the idea of being inclusive as well as to that of getting to a truth beyond the regularly announced ones, so stylistic "experiment," if that's what it was, anyway stylistic variety, seemed a good way to get what I wanted.

The first way I wrote that felt completely my own to me was the style of *When the Sun Tries to Go On*. When I wrote that poem I felt positively bardic; I felt that I had come upon a new use for words, a means of communication that enabled me to say things never said before. I sat in my one-room apartment on Charles Street in New York and wrote this poem every day for three months. Several times I remember my heart beating so fast that I was afraid I was going to die. I never supposed many people aside from Frank who seemed to love it would catch on to and like my poem, it just kept paddling me along through those spring days of 1951. The "rules" (not conscious to me but practiced), as I look back on them now, were something like these: don't "make sense" in an ordinary way; don't make sense in a Joycean way; don't make non-sense in a Steinian way; make a sense you never heard before, if you understand how you're doing it you're not doing it right; no puns; no jokes; no hidden meanings. There were "meanings" of course,

> near "to be"
> An angel is shouting, "Wilder baskets!"

I suppose it could be thought of as funny (inappropriately low) that an angel would *shout,* as well as that he would shout something as apparently unclear (unclear in the sense of unfamiliar) as "wilder baskets"; however I've always felt perfectly happy with the metaphysical implications of this description, which has the advantage of letting me bring in angels without completely believing in them but believing in the idea "angels"; and if there could be such beings, would they find "mere being" enough or urge us on to "Wilder baskets"?

This *Sun Tries to Go On* style I tried to hang on to for a while after I seemed to have nothing more to say in it. It was hard to believe I'd ever be done with it. For a time I thought that like some intense obsessed painters I might be able to go on that way forever. One thing that happened is I fell in love and suddenly found myself using that Sun-style to be more or less clear, at least syntactically and rhetorically—

> It's the ocean of Western steel
> Bugles that makes me want to listen
> To the parting of the trees,
> Like intemperate smiles . . .

Next was the style of most of the poems in *Thank You.* Then I wrote *Ko,* which was quite different from these earlier styles—in the first place, it rhymed, which I had hardly done before, it was in stanzas, and it told a story. Storytelling was a great find. Writing *Ko* I went on what seemed a wonderful binge of storytelling—love stories, adventure stories, crime stories, sports stories, all kinds, some speeded up, some slowed down, long, short, full of all kinds of details. There were four or five stories going on at the same time (as in Ariosto). Nothing in the stories was thought out in advance; with my rhyme scheme *ababab cc* and the happy Tuscan spring weather, I just let the stories "happen"—the need to rhyme had a lot of effect on the action. I didn't comment, didn't psychologize or analyze in any way, my main demand being that I be surprised and delighted by what happened. Then, too, to stay in the poem, a passage had to surprise and delight me one week, one month later as well. In letting the stories unravel, as it were all by themselves, by avoiding any planned stories, any stories that had a point to make, I thought I might come on a true story or two, something that could be true in a way regular stories weren't. Writing about this time in *Seasons on Earth* I described this idea I had then as a belief that

> The truth might lie in the right mix of actions
> . . . .
> Such sequences, perhaps, if gotten right,
> Might find the truth, as flowers find the light.

I was extremely excited and pleased by a review of *Ko,* which I misinterpreted. The author of this brief review wrote that *Ko* was a "true tale," and I thought, Yes, somebody caught on to it, and I've actually done it, written a story that goes beyond plain stories and tells a *true* one. Of course what the reviewer meant was not that, but simply that my poem really told a story and wasn't just a symbolic or impressionistic narrative "front." Well that was okay but not what gave me that sudden gust of glory (for a few minutes). Later there were the instructional poems in *The Art of Love,* influenced as I've said, by my teaching. These poems were very flat and plain and about as far as possible from *When the Sun Tries to Go On,* but I guess you could say the two were alike in both being extreme.

I felt again, writing *On the Edge,* that I had found the secret, at last the form or style in which I could say everything and anything, as I had felt before, writing *When the Sun Tries to Go On* and again writing *Ko* and *The Art of Love* and again, later, writing *The First Step.* In *On the Edge,* which is autobiographical, the dissociations (or whatever they are) have most to do with re-creating (in a precise way) past moments—

The journal of I forget

O "scatalogue"

The pink air was guzzly a little and fashionable

I was writing as if a little to the side, trying to get the main things and feelings but not committing my lines to instances so specific that they'd weigh them down. As in

Martin McScrumbold who controlled the sedge
For fifteen companies of marble fusions

in which I want to get a little mixed-up music out of big business.

Prose (fiction) was a great treat to write when I finally found a way to do it—in my novel *The Red Robins*—opening up, as it did, what seemed uncountable new varieties of how to put words together. One of the main inspirations for this book (*The Red Robins*) were a couple of books, perhaps not totally "bad" but certainly written to a nonliterary audience for presumably commercial purposes, by a writer whose pseudonym was Warner Fabian—the books were *Flaming Youth* and *Summer Bachelors*. The mix of behavioral and syntactical simplicity with an atmosphere constantly perfumed with sexual innuendo—it was even better than *Love Comics*, which I also liked. Boys' airplane books, Hardy Boys stories, and others of that genre were in back of it, too. I didn't feel close to any of the writers of minimalist or absurdist prose, though Don Barthelme was kind enough to include me in collections with them. I felt a lot closer to *Fantomas;* I read three or four volumes of it. I didn't see Roy Lichtenstein's comic-strip paintings (he hadn't painted them yet) till I was about five years into the novel, but when I did see them they were encouraging. I admired some of Don Barthelme's sentences. The way they started out in one place and ended you up entirely in another, all the while including some bitter parody or other or some little intense bit of sensuality. I already knew, of course, Proust's sentences, those phenomenally tidal things. Later, too late to use in *The Red Robins* but in time for my stories in *Hotel Lambosa* I discovered Viktor Shklovsky, Leonardo Sciascia, Isaak Babel, and Yasunari Kawabata. Later still I found Jim Salter's sentences and he told me to look in *Out of Africa* and there are great sentences there. I know that sentences alone don't make good stories but I was interested in paying attention to them in a particular way. When I wrote *Hotel Lambosa* I wanted to write in a way just about completely unlike that of *The Red Robins*—"real prose" not "poetic" in the way the *Robins* might be said to be. The sentences there aren't the same but I still wanted them to surprise and to snap around suddenly like a not necessarily unfriendly snake. St.-John Perse's sentences were an inspiration for the *The Red Robins'* prose—they had an "elevation," a wonderful twentieth-century French operatic elevation, subtler and more perfumed and nuanced even than Whitman's. Oh, another influence on its prose were the early short stories of Pasternak and his autobiography *Safe Conduct*. Pasternak wrote sentences that took me by surprise with every word and I'd never seen anything like them. I was also interested in different ways of going from one sentence to another—in both *The Red Robins* and in the *Hotel Lambosa*.

The Comic

Some readers think of a poem as a sort of ceremony—a funeral, a wedding—where anything comic is out of order. They expect certain feelings to be touched on in certain conventional ways. Dissociation, even obscurity, may be tolerated, but only as long as the tone remains solemn or sad enough. (This is why John [Ashbery] gets away with a lot of craziness, I believe.) Frank O'Hara's comic technique is aerated by a feeling of vivacity and variety. I love the quality in Frank's work that makes its message always that life is so rich, so full of variety and excitement that one would be crazy to think that anything else was the theme and crazier not to participate in it as much as one could, "to live / as variously as possible"

What spanking opossums of sneaks are caressing the routes!

This cartoon-comedy vision of sneaker possums sexily spanking their way down the highway positively sings and fizzes with something—without which poetry is something a lot less than it could be. The comic, in a poet like O'Hara or Wallace Stevens or Byron, Aristophanes, Shakespeare, Lautréamont, Max Jacob, is a part of what is most serious for art to get to—ecstasy, unity, freedom, completeness, dionysiac things. One can get a hint of this ecstasy, a whiff from these heights even in a small parody, in one funny line somebody writes. There may be a perfectly serious poem, a good poem ("Resolution and Independence," for example) and some other person writes a parody of it and one line of the parody may have more truth than the whole original poem, or at least be freer to reach the intoxicating heights that sometimes seem where truth is from. One (rather tedious) view of the comic is that it is the absurd, that means that the comic work is always *referring* to the ordinary world and to the ordinary ideas about it. The comic writer, the idea is, is comic because he thought the world sweet but has found it bitter and meaningless. There are some works like this but not great or the best things. Satire is wonderful and one needs it. Absurdity perhaps not. I guess it had its time. In any case, it's the "true tale" uses of the comic that interest me most.

The comic in our own time is probably slightly different from what it used to be. Look at Picasso, for example, Max Ernst ("Two Children Frightened by a Nightingale"). One contemporary comic effect comes from a sort of unconscious or irrational letting go, saying whatever comes into your head in the interests of surprise. Or letting change do it, as in the games the surrealists played

Le cadavre exquis boira le vin nouveau

I love the combination of the comic and the sensuous-sexy with a mild air of wisdom all around in Ariosto and in Byron.

Ambitions

Do I still really believe in the poetic ambitions I've been talking about—about getting to the sublime, ecstasy, the truth. Well, I still *write* as if I do; I still believe in the poetry. And it's what shows me the life I want to go on having. To have it properly I have to go on writing more. One's own poems (those of others, too? probably less rapidly so) wear out. Somewhat. Once when I asked Frank why, he thought (we were very young), we wrote poetry he said Have you looked recently at any of the poetry that's already been written. ("Another filthy page of poetry," he said he wanted to write. There was a man!) I imagine now, for the first time, that his answer to me included the poems that he and I had already written.

The New York School

The New York School? You want me before we stop to come back to the New York School? We were very close friends, John, Frank, and I, and poetry was a big part of it. Being together so much and talking so much and writing poems and showing them to each other so much and telling each other what to read so much and all of that, we were a little bit, I suppose, like the members of a team, like the Yankees or the Minnesota Vikings. We inspired each other, we envied each other, we emulated each other, we were very critical of each other, we admired each other, we were almost entirely dependent on each other for support. Each had to be better than the others but if one flopped we all did. I used to have the fantasy that I was the middle number of this dynamic trio, John all prophesy and the sublime, Frank all excited conversation and the streets, I somewhere in between, a more "physical" Ashbery, a more "poetic" O'Hara. I have no idea what they thought—if anything—in this regard. But I remember when I wrote and published, in *Poetry,* one of my excited, conversational (sort of) poems to Marina, "In Love with You," John wrote to me (I was in France), "Your poem in *Poetry* is beautiful. But have you gone over to Frank completely?" Or maybe what he wrote was, "But it seems an awful lot like Frank." Was John afraid of being left behind at Delphos while Frank and I skateboarded off into the urban sunrise? I don't think so. The most remarkable thing I can remember about John's and Frank's poetry then is that it didn't have in it anything I *dis*liked. Every piece of paper either handed me to read was welcome, like a wonderful lemonade in the scorching summer of our postadolescent souls. We had little resistance to each other's work, as one might have little resistance to heat or to cold. I've loved other writers—Max Jacob, Éluard, Byron, etc.—but I haven't known them. They weren't there, at the bar or in the studio or on the phone; they weren't fellow Vikings, shoving me around. What was may be really alike in our poems it's harder to say. I used to say, Very important to all of us was the surface of the language. It does seem that whatever our poems had to say, the words got there first. But that may have been only my impression.

UNDER DISCUSSION
David Lehman, General Editor
Donald Hall, Founding Editor

Volumes in the Under Discussion series collect reviews and essays about individual poets. The series is concerned with contemporary American and English poets about whom the consensus has not yet been formed and the final vote has not been taken. Titles in the series include: